D0114581

The Coldest War

Books by C. L. Sulzberger

The Coldest War: Russia's Game in China   *1974*
An Age of Mediocrity   *1973*
Unconquered Souls: The Resistentialists   *1973*
The Tooth Merchant   *1973*
The Last of the Giants   *1970*
A Long Row of Candles   *1969*
American Heritage History of World War II   *1966*
Unfinished Revolution: America and
   the Third World   *1965*
The Test: De Gaulle and Algeria   *1962*
My Brother Death   *1961*
What's Wrong with U.S. Foreign Policy   *1959*
The Big Thaw   *1956*
Sit-down with John L. Lewis   *1938*

C. L. Sulzberger

The Coldest War

Russia's Game in China

Harcourt Brace Jovanovich
New York and London

Printed in the United States of America

Library of Congress Cataloging in Publication Data

Sulzberger, Cyrus Leo, 1912–
   The coldest war.

   1. China—Foreign relations—Russia.   2. Russia—
Foreign relations—China.   3. China—Politics and
government—1949–   I. Title.
DS740.R8S96   327.51′047   74-1466
ISBN 0-15-118979-X
ISBN 0-15-618500-8 (pbk.)

A B C D E F G H I J

For David Bruce

the last eighteenth-century American,
with admiration, gratitude, and affection

Acknowledgment

I wish to thank the New York *Times* for permission to publish in this book material from some of my columns. I also wish to thank Isabel Bass and Linda Lamarche for help in preparation of the manuscript.

CLS

Contents

1

The Origin of the Quarrel

The first Sino-Russian negotiation took place in the seventeenth century at Nerchinsk, in eastern Siberia. The Russians were represented by a Pole, and the Chinese by two Jesuits. The envoys all spoke Latin. Today, three centuries later, the two giant neighbors have yet to discover a common language or a common policy.

The Chinese, who consider themselves good Marxist-Leninists, must read with wry cynicism what Lenin wrote in 1900: "The greedy paws of the European capitalists have reached out into China, and almost the first to do so was the Russian government which now swears to its 'unselfishness.' "

One of the main factors contributing to the tension between Communism's two behemoths is land. On July 10, 1964, Chairman Mao declared: "One hundred years ago, the region east of Baikal became Russian territory and later on Vladivostok, Khabarovsk, Kamchatka and other regions became the territory of the Soviet Union. We have not yet presented the bill for this list."

Nevertheless, Peking today stipulates that it has no major territorial pretensions and merely wishes to renegotiate the nineteenth-century land treaties it considers were unfairly imposed. "The Sino-Soviet boundary question," says Premier Chou En-lai, "should be settled peacefully through negotiations free from any threat." Yet on April 2, 1973, the Chinese army's Fukien Front Radio claimed the Russians had annexed 1,500,000 square kilometers from China between 1858 and 1881.

However, Peking does not feel that today, with Russia's vast army deployed along the border of People's China, there is any chance of exploring the question on a basis "free from any threat." For their part, the Chinese are prepared to make minor accommodations such as pulling troops back if the Russians follow suit.

But they want no significant treaty yet, and anyway, having seen Russia seize its own ally Czechoslovakia in 1968, they regard treaties with some skepticism. China is digging in and playing for time.

Sino-Soviet differences are not limited to geography. As early as 1927, when Borodin was Stalin's adviser with the Chinese Communists, Mao Tse-tung was urging that his country's revolution be based on peasant support, a doctrine by then considered heretical in Moscow, although Lenin himself had espoused it earlier. Indeed, it was partly as a result of Soviet pressure that Mao was excluded from the Chinese Politburo.

Despite a temporary Sino-Soviet alliance, the triumph of Maoist Communism in China clearly disgruntled the Soviet Union. Their ideological differences were irreconcilable, and the dispute became global.

The Russians now called the Chinese "dogmatists" and the Chinese called the Russians "revisionists." Peking claimed that Moscow was encouraging dissident movements, above all those led by Liu Shao-chi, once head of the People's Republic, and by Lin Piao, who had been constitutionally designated as Chairman Mao's successor but who was to die in ignominy, fleeing after an abortive coup attempt.

Liu, who represented urban influences, had spent some years in Russia, as had Lin, who was cured of tuberculosis in Leningrad just before World War II. While there is no detailed evidence linking them to Kremlin machinations, Liu did favor reactivation of the Sino-Soviet alliance, and Lin is thought to have opposed China's new friendship with the United States. Chou En-lai now denounces Liu's "revisionist" line and maintains that Lin died fleeing "as a defector to the Soviet revisionists in betrayal of the party and the country."

Thus the clash between Russia and China is territorial, ideological, political, and increasingly military. China believes that if it had given aid to Pakistan in the 1971 Indian war, Russia would have attacked on India's behalf. China sees India and Outer Mongolia as vassals of Russia and fears Brezhnev's policy of seeking to encircle China.

China remembers with bitterness Khrushchev's 1959 failure to send a promised "sample atom bomb" and with even more bitterness the withdrawal of all Soviet technicians and planners one year later. And it deeply resents construction of an implacable Soviet military machine on its own borders.

What China fears most are plots inside the republic. Premier Chou recalled to a recent party congress this prophecy on the part of a "chief of the Soviet revisionists": "Sooner or later the healthy forces expressing the true interests of China will have their decisive say."

For Chou these words imply "reducing China to a colony of Soviet revisionist social-imperialism," because "enemies at home and abroad all understand that the easiest way to capture a fortress is from within. . . . Lin Piao will appear again and so will persons like Liu Shaochi." Thus, while the rest of the world talks blithely of détente, China finds itself engaged in the coldest war of all with Russia.

For the most part, neither Russia nor China has any ironclad, simon-pure right to the contested areas, which were almost all originally occupied by Central or East Asian tribes with no racial or linguistic connection to either the Slavs or the Han Chinese.

Nevertheless, these areas were of enormous strategic importance, especially the vast region known as Turkestan, which is still divided into Soviet Central Asia and China's Sinkiang autonomous province, a region described by the inventor of modern geopolitics, Sir Halford Mackinder, as the world's "heartland." But if this heartland was originally dominated by Altaic and Sinic peoples, generally nomads, their protostates, once independent countries like Khiva, Bokhara, Kokandia, or Kashgaria, have largely vanished into the history books. And it was only natural that as Russia and China asserted their control, they would be brought into immediate and proximate rivalry.

This rivalry, now coming to a head, is of immensely greater importance to the political development of the globe than the sordid Watergate scandal now straining America's democratic governance, or the endless war between Arabs and Israelis over the Palestine succession and the consequent petroleum cutoff and world-wide energy crisis.

When historians in the year 2000 look back on the final quarter of this century, they will see that it was the present Sino-Soviet relationship that shaped their world.

The territorial quarrel has received the greatest attention because actual fighting has broken out along Russia's and China's frontier, the earth's longest border between neighboring countries, but it is not the only difference contributing to the strain. Ideological fissures and disputes of an almost religious nature on how Marxist-Leninist Communism should be interpreted and applied; ever-sharper political rivalry for influence in the Third World of developing nations (and also, incidentally, for influence in Japan); the Soviet fear that if China is allowed to industrialize and remilitarize unchecked, it will become impossible to face down; China's old racist tendency to view foreigners as "barbarians" playing one role and Russia's new racist tendency to mutter about a "yellow menace" playing another role; and, finally, demography—the Soviet anxiety that a massive Chinese population, already some 800 million, will seek to press into the relatively vacant spaces of Siberia, Uzbekistan, and Kazakhstan—all these factors, some of them going back for decades, have led to exorbitantly expensive military confrontations, passionately hostile propaganda, and a bitter sectarian rivalry within the Marxist fold. Moscow has contrived to improve its relations with its western neighbors and the United States while shifting more and more of its armed forces and defense investment eastward; in the same manner, Peking is seeking Occidental friends while allocating an unreasonable amount, given its limited funds, to a defense program aimed solely at the U.S.S.R. and including everything from mounting a nuclear-missile arsenal to the construction of the most gigantic expanse of tunnel the history of engineering has ever known, as a protection against possible atomic attack.

European statesmen became concerned with the gradual development of enmity between Russia and China far earlier than their American counterparts. Indeed, they cautioned Washington against choosing sides between the two Communist giants long before President Nixon and Henry Kissinger instituted the new Pentagonal basis for American global diplomacy (Russia, China, Japan, Western Europe).

The U.S. was still fulminating about a "Sino-Soviet bloc" years after the vestiges of that alliance had themselves split into hostile halves. In 1966, at the Pearl Harbor headquarters of the American commander in chief for the entire Pacific area, which included everything from Japan to Australia and from Honolulu to Burma, I had the mission of the command officially defined for me— indeed, flashed at me from a screen—as a mission to maintain "a forward strategy on the periphery of the Sino-Soviet bloc in the western Pacific."

Yet the whole rest of the world already knew that the Russians and Chinese were no longer even friends, let alone allies. And this knowledge was taken into the policy-making considerations of almost every capital but Washington. Old Konrad Adenauer told me in Bonn in February 1965:

"My policy has always been based upon the two following ideas. The relationship between Russia and China would develop in such a way that Russia would be pleased to have no enemies in the West and would therefore feel free to turn its attention increasingly toward the East. Secondly I felt it was quite obvious that the Soviet Union was having increasing economic difficulties. I thought it would be folly to help Russia solve these economic difficulties unless the Russians made concessions on their side.

"Unfortunately the democracies have not taken advantage of the latter situation. First the British Conservative government sent supplies to the Russians. Then the Americans sent their wheat, asking for no counter-concessions. This was a capital folly on the part of the British and the Americans. It makes it much easier for a dictatorship to produce a foreign policy in such circumstances. A dictatorship can avoid internal economic pressure. But the businessmen in a democracy want to make money and that is dominant. Then they put pressure on their government. First this happened in Britain, then in America, then in France. Now the same thing is being repeated as our own industry exerts pressure on our government. Don't make any mistake. I don't want the Russians to starve. But I see no reason to send them factories unless they make concessions to us in exchange."

French President Charles de Gaulle, too, had for years been fascinated by the rise of China. In July 1965, I told him that I had always been puzzled by his reference to a Europe "from the Atlantic to the Urals." I recognized, of course, that the Urals were the conventional geographical boundary between Europe and Asia, but I wanted to know if he was speaking politically as well.

"I recognize that this phrase irritates the Russians," he answered, "but that is their affair, not mine. The real

Russia stops at the Urals. All the rest—Turkestan, Siberia, parts of Mongolia—these are all colonies. Colonies colonized by the Russians.

"And probably, almost surely, in the future they will become a part of China. China has 700 million people. It is not a great power today. But in twenty years it will be a great power, and in fifty years it will be an enormous power. The Russians know this well—and so do the Chinese. This is the inner basis of their quarrel. Of course, being Communists, they always put everything on an ideological basis. But the truth is the opposition between Russia and China has national origins."

A year and a half later, I asked him again whether he thought China would ever be a superpower. "Certainly," he said, without the slightest hesitation, "but in thirty years. And when this happens China will make claims against everybody, against the whole world, but above all against Russia. China will make claims against India. It will insist on expelling United States influence from Formosa, from South Korea, and it will even insist on removing your protectorate from Japan. But Russia, the Soviets, will feel tremendous pressure."

In 1968, De Gaulle said to me: "I remember a very characteristic phrase of Chou En-lai's. Someone had asked him if he did not think everything must be done to avoid the suffering caused by war. He replied that, on the contrary, it was by war that big things were achieved. He said China had become what it is today as a result of invasion, destruction, and suffering. This philosophical attitude is very impressive and I am afraid it remains a factor in Chinese policy."

Thus, while a long list of foreign observers assumed that Russia and China would one day split, the religiously anti-Communist U.S. State Department was still too befuddled by the Manichaean legacy of John Foster Dulles to take this in.

Edgar Faure, the former French premier, who had visited China in the early 1960's, came to believe that Khrushchev had been dismissed because both the Soviet and the Chinese Communist party hierarchies feared that he wanted an outright split between the two neighbors. At that time both were prepared for a separation, but not for a divorce.

Divorce was inevitable, however. Marshal Tito told me, when he was working to resume friendly relations with Moscow, that "as soon as Trotsky's idea of the permanent revolution was defeated, it became evident that there were different roads to socialism. Nowadays only China wants one road to socialism."

As for the Russians themselves, on January 22, 1964, Sergei Vinogradov, Soviet ambassador to Paris and one of the Kremlin's ablest diplomats, assured me that Mao Tse-tung was a far worse despot "even than Stalin" and that whoever raised his voice against the government had "his head knocked off." The Chinese lived in misery, he said; economically, the country was a shambles. They were racists and hated every white man. He added that it was not just a legend, that—although he could not reveal his source—he knew it for a fact that Mao had said he wasn't worried about another war because, whatever happened, 300 million Chinese could survive, and rule the world.

I asked Vinogradov if he was concerned that France might help China develop nuclear weapons. He admitted that Russia was very concerned about this, "just like the United States," and asked if I thought the French had a thermonuclear weapon. I said I did not think they would for eighteen months. He said that Russia had no intention of helping China develop nuclear weapons, and that perhaps that was why the Chinese hated them even more than they hated the Americans.

Etienne Manac'h, who was then head of the Asian division of the French Foreign Ministry and who was later to be named ambassador to China, told me early in 1967 that Brezhnev informed the Polish government that Russia was openly supporting Liu Shao-chi and his faction of the Chinese party against both Mao Tse-tung and Lin Piao, and that it was clear a war of succession to Mao had already begun between Liu and Lin. Yet old Mao not only survived the contest, but also purged each of the contenders, charging them, one after the other, with plotting on behalf of Moscow.

Maurice Schumann, France's foreign minister, who had been received by both Mao and Chou in Peking, told me in August 1969 that he could not imagine China starting a war with Russia in the foreseeable future. And the Russians, he said, would not dare to start a war with China without the guarantee of a quiet situation in Europe. The Russians could never forget that their revolution started partly in consequence of their weakness in Asia, in the Japanese war of 1905. He was certain the Russians did not want to touch off any conflict without having some sort of gentlemen's agreement with the United States—and this, he thought, was wholly unlikely.

Nevertheless, the twin possibility of a war touched off by Russia's fears of and irritation with China and waged to insure that Mao would be succeeded by a leader favorable to Kremlin policies became increasingly a subject of discussion in foreign chanceries. André Malraux, the writer and former Gaullist minister of culture, who knew China forty years ago and who had also recently talked with Mao and Chou, assured me Mao had said to him in December 1966: "We—people like De Gaulle and myself—have no successors."

Malraux maintained that no one knew what would happen in China when Mao died, that Chou wanted only to administer policy and had no ambition to succeed him. There might be a civil war of succession; there would almost surely be some bloodshed. Only a reckless prophet could predict the outcome. Malraux found Mao convinced that whatever had to be done in China had to be done by him alone.

Time, implacable time, has become the crucial factor of the Maoist revolution in People's China today: those old men, Mao and Chou, hear its winged chariot hurrying near.

2

A Different
Revolution

It was inevitable that the Chinese Communist revolution would develop differently from that of Russia, or indeed from that of any other country. First of all, China is the world's most ancient continuing independent culture and society, founded in 2205 B.C. by the Hsia dynasty. Egypt may be older, but its continuity was often interrupted and it enjoyed a comparable influence only in the days of the Pharaohs. So a Sinic element was perforce and inescapably introduced into the Marxist mixture cooked by Mao Tse-tung.

If in Greece there had been pure glory based on a harmony of sky, sea, and earth; in Rome, an imposing grandeur, founded on order and organization; in China there was a splendor, variegated and often gaudy, marked by inventiveness, indeed by boundless imagination. It was the Chinese who invented silk cloth, porcelain, gunpowder, the seismograph, the astrolabe, the compass, the crossbow.

When Marco Polo came to Hangchow at the end of the thirteenth century, it had a population of 900,000 and was, he wrote, "the greatest city which may be found in the world, where so many pleasures may be found that one fancies himself to be in paradise." Some years later, Odoric da Pordenone described it as a city "greater than any in the world."

The venerable capital, Sian, where artists molded for Tang emperors horses equal to those created by the Greeks, in marble (or, by the earlier Hans, in bronze), still contains a forest of stone steles recording events that otherwise might be forgotten. One slab even tells the story of a Nestorian priest who came from the West to found the first Christian chapel in China, 1,200 years ago.

Beneath a mound in central Shensi province, close to China's cultural roots, archaeologists have discovered the tomb of the beautiful Princess Yung Tai, who died young and brokenhearted after her husband's execution: when her loving father mounted the Imperial Dragon throne, he brought her body from a distant grave to Shensi. There, painted along the tomb's underground walls to commemorate the lords and ladies who mourned with him the unfortunate girl, were frescoes surpassing those in contemporary Italy.

In Tatung, the grim northern coal town where the occupying Japanese committed some of the greatest atrocities of World War II in casting miners without number into what are now known as "ten-thousand-man pits," are some of China's greatest treasures, which few foreigners have been allowed to see in recent years. The intricate story of Buddhism, introduced into China by Indian monks, is told in the two Hwayen monastery temples, with their extraordinary wall paintings, massive statues, and library of wood-block-printed scriptures, all beneath ceilings set with panels resembling those of *quattrocento* Florence.

And outside the city, amid sandstone escarpments, a series of caves reminiscent of Egypt's Valley of the Kings was carved out of the sheer cliff face in the fifth century. No fewer than 51,000 statues, large and small, were cut from the rock or molded in plaster to honor the various Buddhas and their saintly attendants.

Even the briefest acquaintance with its seemingly interminable scroll reminds one that Chinese civilization has continuously renewed itself since the Neolithic age. One can see literally reflected on the walls of palaces and temples the germinal moments of decline, followed by foreign conquest.

This is true not only in regard to the Mongol and Manchu dynasties, which rode clattering in from the north, but above all in regard to the final Ching dynasty, which ended in Sun Yat-sen's revolution of 1911 and led eventually to the dynamic People's Republic of Mao Tse-tung.

The decline in taste and judgment, the decadence, stares blankly from the final Ching relics of a 4,000-year-old imperial epoch whose miserable masses staggered into the twentieth century, the men in ridiculous pigtails, the women with painfully deformed bound feet. Art has a way of mirroring the health of a society: one has only to think back to Greece and Rome.

One therefore asks oneself, when regarding the Stalinist architecture that squats beside the broad avenues of revolutionary China's cities and listening to endless hortatory slogans and propaganda—in literature, music, ballet, and the theater—if this redundant clamor is really necessary to achieve the goal of greatness sought by the vigorous People's Republic.

Perhaps the answer is yes. Yet pondering the esthetic panoply of forty centuries of Chinese history, one doubts it. In any case, the answer will not be quick in coming, for one of the splendors of China is its implacable patience.

It is exceedingly difficult for a foreigner to penetrate this wall of patience. During a recent visit to the People's Republic, I recalled the advice of the great French Jesuit and Sinologue Teilhard de Chardin to a Shanghai friend: "Write about China before you have been there too long; later you would break your pen." (Now, having broken my typewriter, I can add another quotation, this time from an old Chinese sage, Chuang-tzu: "He who knows that he is a fool is not a great fool." At least I know I am a fool to write about China, whose language I do not speak, whose books or newspapers I cannot read, whose immense history I cannot pretend to know, and where I have no well-informed Chinese friends given to frank confidences.)

Most visitors have a difficult time in contemporary

China. Many Chinese who could speak foreign languages were eliminated during the revolution. There are few with whom it is possible to make contact, and they have all been officially designated.

Moreover, there is a limited number of visas issued to foreigners who, unlike me, speak fluent Chinese—unless they have already shown themselves sympathetic to Maoism. The lack of interpreters, the scarcity of accommodation, and the ever-present bureaucratic red tape all make it hard to get around.

But once the foreigner is there, he is smothered with kindness, although excessive kindness can become an effective form of isolation. Contact with the outside world is tenuous. I had to learn about the Middle East war in Shanghai accidentally, by encountering some foreign diplomats, although I had been hourly attended by functionaries who surely read their newspapers.

When the tourist is a visiting correspondent, he is handled under a special protocol. His desires are all listened to with sympathetic interest. Then he is sent to visit chosen places and personalities chosen for him, often on the far side of his original requests.

I was not surprised to hear my guide in Yenan brightly advise me that he had taken "Mr. Marquis Childs" on a similar tour. In Peking I asked Chen Chung, of the Agriculture Ministry, if he had seen any U.S. farmers. "Mr. Joseph Alsop," he replied with a happy grin. I grinned, too.

Many places, like the Great Mosque of Sian, which I eventually saw, are described as "inconvenient" or "closed for repairs." Information and statistics supplied by "experts" vary.

My wife asked officials in a children's crèche how orphans were cared for. She was told, first, that there are no orphans in China, and then, as an afterthought, that, yes, there were four parentless youngsters, whom Premier

Chou En-lai himself had helped. Maybe "orphan" means something different in Chinese!

Under such a system, truth cannot escape from figuring on the casualty lists. Chinese officials told me they do not consider Western journalists "objective"; but they do their best to make sure we cannot be.

It is hard to interpret some concepts. When I was told that Lu Hsun, a left-wing but non-Communist writer who died in 1936, was much admired, I asked if other non-Marxist artists were respected also. For example, could one accidentally discover the name of a sculptor of the famous Han (bronze) or Tang (porcelain) horses? The reply: "Only if it were shown he made a contribution to mankind." "Isn't beauty a contribution?" Silence.

A kind of one-upmanship is encouraged among visitors: you are the first to go here or there. This is an odd ploy to resort to for a nation that has been on the regular Western curiosity path for at least twelve centuries. I can boast only that I am the first American columnist over sixty to visit Inner Mongolia since 1949, and the first ever with a Greek wife to lunch in Chengchow.

A visiting journalist seems to have to wait until the end of his trip before being permitted to see important personages—like the soup that terminates a good Chinese banquet. This tactic produces quite a propaganda harvest, since few correspondents wish to forfeit these appointments by writing too bluntly. From the start, Chuang-tzu's fools, like me, are forced to become instant pundits on unfamiliar subjects—without giving excessive offense.

When that delicious terminal soup does come, the conversation is subtly conducted according to magnificently prepared briefings. In my case, Premier Chou laced his great personal charm with quotations from my own writings; for example, "In the phrase you made famous in your column . . ." He is very persuasive.

Surely, no Westerner, by definition ill-prepared (he

lacks language, background, cultural roots, and a comparable tradition of historical grandeur and national suffering), can hope to approach with sufficient understanding the immensity of China, its heritage, its aspirations. Yet it is this very impossibility that is thrust upon one.

The Chinese revolution was the most important consequence of World War II, just as the Russian revolution was the most important consequence of World War I. Each was Marxist, violent, and triumphant only after a bloody civil conflict and successive ideological purges. Also, each chose a different road. China based itself as firmly on the dreams and requirements of the agricultural peasantry as Russia had on the aspirations of the industrial workers.

The monumental significance of the new China lies in its thrust for change and in the remarkable durability of Chairman Mao and his chief lieutenant, Chou.

Although Mao is over eighty and Chou is over seventy-five, they remain in command of their fascinating country's destiny. It is as if Lenin, the first brilliantly successful Marxist practitioner, had still been governing the Soviet Union in 1941 when it was invaded by Nazi Germany.

When Chairman Mao assumed control of all China a quarter of a century ago, it was in far worse shape than the Russia relinquished by the czars. The ideology bequeathed by Sun Yat-sen's uprising was diffuse and confused. The China of 1949 was a land of clans and war lords; of famine, beggars, alternating floods and droughts, typhus, plague, and, above all, humiliated, ruined peasants, saddled with the corruption of a disintegrating feudal system.

The Maoist revolution gave this China nationhood, dignity, and pride. Even a swift glimpse of it affirms the wisdom of Teilhard de Chardin. One can write at least that much without breaking one's pen.

When Maoism came to power, China was poorer than Pakistan, India, or Indonesia, with a per-capita food ration

one-fifth of France's and an average longevity less than
half that of the United States. Yet today it is a vibrant
power, struggling slowly but successfully to create a better
life for its people; they are for the first time adequately
clothed and fed, proud of their international status, over-
whelmingly literate and healthy, and confident of the future.

As in all mass upheavals, these achievements cost a
heavy price in blood and suffering. But Maoism has refused to copy either the fat-dripping West or dogmatic
Russia, and has resolutely followed its own road, economically and politically.

And now, ignoring both superpower blocs, China is
forging its leadership of the underdeveloped Third World.
It may be a nation still mounted on bicycles, but it is also
a nation initiated into the secrets of the atomic-missile age.

Mao's two great innovative contributions were to base
China's society on peasants, rather than on technicians,
workers, or traditional intellectuals, and to accept the need
for a permanent revolution that would renew itself cycli-
cally. The latter is a most radical thesis indeed, transcending Thomas Jefferson's untested belief that the tree of
liberty must from time to time refresh itself with the blood
of tyrants. Mao sees that victorious revolutions create
their own elite, what Djilas called the New Class.

Mao therefore has determined that, whenever necessary,
each successive new class must be uprooted and discarded.
As he told an Albanian delegation seven years ago: "The
building of socialism cannot be accomplished in one, two,
three or four cultural revolutions. There must be many
others."

But as China faces this almost endless do-it-yourself
revolution, aware that ceaseless movement carries with it
the risk of ceaseless instability, it is also aware that this is
the price of progress on a scale the world has not hitherto
known.

China experimented with many facets of what is now

called "Marxism" long before Marx himself ever lived. The current attacks on the Confucian philosophy show that Maoism has its roots in old concepts. Even the thought of autarky and state management of society is not novel. Chancellor Wang An-shih recommended to the medieval emperor Tai-tsu that "the state should take the entire management of commerce, industry and agriculture into its own hands, with a view to succoring the working classes and preventing them from being ground into dust by the rich."

Given its centuries-old habits of government and its essential poverty, China has developed a rather anti-individualist concept of society. Community interests have often prevailed, at least in the intermittent epochs of good administration.

Common sense, group opinion, and pragmatic worth have tended to hold a higher place in China than abstract ideals. Opportunism does not necessarily conflict with conscience. Nor have the Chinese been known for their religious piety. Long before the Maoist revolution, the frontiers of rival faiths and philosophies were ill-defined. Public life may have been paved with ceremony but it was always roofed with superstition.

Even now it is hard to distinguish in the Maoist credo what is original with Chairman Mao, what has been adapted from other versions of Marxism, and what has merely been updated from China's heritage. The heart of Maoism today is a self-imposed seething movement, in which people are plucked from privileged positions and immersed in the tough rural life; whether this will ultimately destroy a social fabric more fragile than suspected remains to be seen.

Chinese leaders encourage this ceaseless ferment for reasons stemming from China's own experience. Its intellectuals have always been distinguished by their contempt for manual labor, and it is clearly useful to destroy such prejudices. But how do the scholars take to carrying human manure in the name of the revolution? And how long will they put up with temporary exile to peasant communes as the price to be paid for their education?

One cannot help feeling kindly disposed toward the earnest, durable Chinese people, still mired in poverty, who started their revolutionary career far behind the rest of the world, who caught up by great effort, but who still have a long way to go. They all work, by government mandate, but one has a feeling that they are wasting a good deal of their time—in part by attending lectures on how to produce.

The Chinese are conditioned to propaganda. One would have thought Chairman Mao had invented the slogan "Dig for Victory" used by Britain's Pioneer Corps in World War II. Even art has become a form of exhortation. There are songs with names like "People's Liberation Army man come and have a cup to tea" and "The brightness of the Tenth Party Congress shines in all our hearts."

A ship captain told me that the red Mao button in his lapel was not a decoration but "a sign of love for the Chairman." As if it were blazingly novel, a factory manager said: "We have organized cadres to make the workers and technicians co-operate."

Yet mass organization has succeeded in original ways. Although you can still see aircraft stewardesses hunting flies with diminutive swatters, the fly has been largely done away with, along with mosquitoes and bedbugs. The plan to eliminate mice has not worked yet, but doubtless will someday.

The Chinese remain easy, engaging people with ready smiles except in large metropolises, like Shanghai, where citizens wear that worried, grumpy look common to residents of big cities everywhere. They are still heavy smokers, garlic-eaters, tea-sippers, and, incidentally, spitters. Cuspidors line hotel corridors. There was even one between us when I talked with Premier Chou En-lai.

The Chinese are today incredibly honest; few of them

lock their doors. Despite their sexless, classless pajama suits, they have not wholly sacrificed their special personality to the god of efficiency. But their revolution has assumed a very particular character.

The only "institutionalized revolution" I had ever heard of before is Mexico's, and that experiment resembles a frozen custard. What Maoist China seeks is to institutionalize the idea of permanent or continuing revolution, which is almost like saying it wants to make dynamism static. Aware that any social upheaval produces a new class of bureaucratic leaders, a class which, like all the others that have preceded it, tends to entrench itself in privilege, the Chinese regime insists on ceaselessly stirring the political mixture, ordering favored people like intellectuals or officials to interrupt their careers and do uncomfortable physical labor in hinterland agricultural communes. There is obviously some discontent, as among students who must spend a few years feeding pigs or carrying buckets of night soil before going from high school to university, and some have chosen to flee the country via Hong Kong.

Nothing quite like such a permanent revolution has ever before been attempted, and therefore it is hard to assess its potential effects. In a way, by insistence on endless bureaucratic upheaval, the ordered search for assured egalitarianism would seem a guarantee of disorder. Indeed, one wonders if the formula is in fact a prescription for institutionalized chaos and if China's new society is strong enough to stand the strain. Chairman Mao forecasts "great disorder" every seven or eight years, but the regime seems prepared to pay the price.

In an oversimplified sense, Maoism sees an elite as ultimately leading to capitalism, and so feels that to attain socialism egalitarianism must be guaranteed. "People are not yet entirely equal," Li Cheng-rei, of the Chinese Academy of Science, told me in Peking. "We have come from a bourgeois society. But in a Communist society there will be true equality."

The chosen method of reaching that objective seems as paradoxical to Western minds as an attempt to square the circle, but Chinese logic and philosophy have always been more flexible. The ancient Taoist creed was based on the assumption that a circle might indeed express the oneness of a cosmos always remaining in a state of flux.

Thus there could be no static conventions. Unceasing interaction of two opposing forces, called "yin" and "yang," one feminine and negative, the other masculine and positive, continually strive against each other and at the same time unite and intertwine. It is not difficult for a nation with this philosophical background to believe politically in a kind of static dynamism.

Nevertheless, the turmoil produced by this system has practical disadvantages as well as theoretical advantages. Egalitarianism is certainly the *mot d'ordre,* as can be seen in the dress, living standards, and shortage of cash one finds throughout People's China.

In the several thousand miles I flew, south, north, west, and east, I was struck by the apparent equality of the national development rate despite previous inequality in various regional take-off levels. The output of consumer goods is still meager, and, apart from emphasis on defense production, there seems almost everywhere to be a concentration on cement, fertilizer, and heavy-industry factories.

But actual output, while statistically impressive compared with that of previous systems, is not astonishingly high, and I am sure that the per-capita productivity is considerably lower than in Western lands, perhaps because low individual productivity makes it easier to keep everyone employed. But a good deal of time is wasted in group discussions, and there is a general feeling of lackadaisical apathy.

How much of this is attributable to psychological factors such as the lack of freedom of choice cannot be estimated. Individual conceptions of freedom have played relatively little role in the evolution of the Chinese personality. And when computer storage banks with the ability to move all citizens up or down the social structure, as permanent revolution requires, become a common feature in Peking, freedom of choice may be forever doomed.

But I venture to say that no human engineering under any social system can permanently dehumanize mankind— which, anyway, is not the goal of Maoism. What the regime wants is to establish a means of raising the masses to an ever higher condition, even if individuals must suffer in the process.

There are many special and individualistic aspects of the Maoist version of Marxism as opposed to the Marxism of, for example, Russia, Rumania, East Germany, or Yugoslavia. One of these aspects, oddly enough, is the modest character of the current outlook of the People's Republic. Modesty is, after all, a most unfamiliar Chinese trait; no nation's rulers have been so haughty for so long. Yet consider:

Some years ago, when visiting an Algerian co-operative near Blida, I was struck by a slogan emblazoned in large letters: "Long Live Revolutionary Modesty." Since revolution is normally dynamic and immodest, this seemed paradoxical.

The Algerian revolution does not claim to mirror the enormous Chinese upheaval, being more pragmatic, less ideological, and on a miniature scale. But the Blida slogan makes more sense in China, where no effort is made to exaggerate the importance of the extraordinary accomplishments.

"China is a big country," Mao Tse-tung is quoted in an official handbook, "but she is still very poor. It will take several decades to make China prosperous." In 1972, the *People's Daily* called the country "relatively backward."

In the communiqué terminating President Nixon's visit, the Chinese stated: "China will never be a superpower."

Chou En-lai told Alain Peyrefitte, the astute head of a French parliamentary delegation, that it would take China at least a hundred years to catch up with the industrially advanced countries.

Chou reminded delegates to the Tenth National Communist Congress: "We are always lagging behind the needs of the objective situation. We still face very heavy tasks in our socialist revolution . . . economically ours is still a poor and developing country."

When I visited the People's Commune of Shuang Chiao, an agricultural collective of 39,000, occupying ninety square kilometers, I was told by the deputy chairman of the Revolutionary Committee, Chuang Ho-shan:

"We started from scratch. We are still imperfect and backward in many ways. We have insufficient mechanization and are really just starting scientific agriculture. But we have a great potential. We must work harder on the line of self-reliance."

Revolutionary modesty is a refreshing and even endearing feature. It contrasts pleasantly with the gigantism and boastfulness of other twentieth-century upheavals, which stressed the size and novelty of their accomplishments, no matter how fanciful. China's is a do-it-yourself revolution that does not intend to rely on either inspiration or assistance from abroad.

Although it has made remarkable advances in twenty-five years and is in the process of overtaking countries that started out with greater economic advantages, the People's Republic, as Mao said, is indeed still poor.

Therefore, despite the former illusions of American policy and despite the torrents of propaganda from the Kremlin, China was right to say that it is not a superpower, although to say that it will "never" be one is unrealistic, in view of the potential of its energetic and intelligent masses. Never is a big word.

Already, through the brilliance of its scientists and technicians, China has entered the atomic-missile club, but it is still a country with no private automobiles, insufficient trucks and buses, and a relatively small aircraft industry. It is a country mostly of bicycle-riders, which is good for the health of its citizens, reduces the menace of pollution, avoids an energy problem, and keeps it from having the traffic nightmare of the West. But it also indicates that mechanization is still rudimentary, except in primordial matters like national defense.

The peasants who were the backbone of the Maoist movement still for the most part caress their endless fields by hand, aided by relatively few and simple tools. They are, as Chuang said, "really just starting scientific agriculture."

So, by deliberately eschewing the role of superpower and showing not even the faintest sign of aggressive intentions, China has moved into the position it politically covets: leader of the Third World. From the dining, the speech-making, the gambei toasts exchanged with distinguished visitors, one might almost say that the Chinese are trying to conquer the Third World by banquets. Since these developing nations comprise the overwhelming majority of the earth and can muster an overwhelming majority in the U.N., China will have a great voice in shaping the world of the future.

Ever since Russia broke with Mao and withdrew its engineers and technicians and embargoed promised materials, China has found it had to solve its problems by itself. This go-it-alone policy has already had impressive results: steel output rose from 5.35 to 23 million tons a year between 1957 and 1972, petroleum from .46 to 29 million tons, and chemical fertilizer from .63 to 20 million tons, despite the fact that emphasis has been on defensive armament. The GNP has increased about 5.5 per cent a year.

To accomplish this, China relied very little on foreign trade, which rose from only $4.265 billion to only $4.611

billion between 1959 and 1971. During this period, it has established a broad industrial base while equalizing individual incomes according to Maoist doctrine.

Agriculture became the economic foundation of China's new basic program, and self-reliance the political cornerstone. And in foreign trade, it was diversification of partners that was stressed.

British Tridents and American Boeings moved in on the heels of Russian Ilyushins and Antonovs as civilian aircraft. Pakistan International Airlines, Air France, Ethiopian Air Lines, and Canadian Pacific joined Russia's Aeroflot as foreign carriers.

And a boat journey along the Shanghai harbor front from the upper Hwang Pu to its confluence with the Yangtze reveals dozens of Rumanian, Somalian, Dutch, Japanese, Singapore, Greek, British, Cypriot, Swedish, Italian, and Liberian ships—but not a single one from the Soviet Union, or the United States, for that matter; American cargoes are sent via Hong Kong or aboard the ships of other nations.

Reflecting national goals, Shanghai, China's principal port, changed quickly from a banking and consuming city to a major industrial producer. I was shown a wide variety of manufactured objects there, including trucks, cars, jeeps, tractors, machine tools, maritime equipment, agricultural machinery, radars, cameras, precision instruments, X-ray machines, artificial lungs, transistors, and telecommunications equipment.

I also visited a shipyard on the riverbank behind a screen of ever-moving junks, their lateen canvas sails stiffened with brown pig's blood. Four 20,000-ton oceangoing vessels have been built here during the last four years.

Wu Kuo-chung, vice-chairman of the yard's Revolutionary Committee, and therefore the equivalent of manager, admitted that "we still have a long way to go. Our shipping industry is young and backward. We have a very low rate of automation, and much of our work is done by hand."

Yet even if there is a relatively low per-capita productivity rate, a nation that has about 800 million people at its disposal, most of whom are in the work force, can enjoy the luxury of comparative lassitude.

I never knew Shanghai in its free-wheeling days, before what is known as the "liberation" of 1949, when Mao revenged himself against Chiang Kai-shek's bloody 1927 Shanghai *Putsch* of Communists, who were then his allies.

The massive old buildings along the harbor front of the former British Concession are now party and administrative headquarters flying red placards emblazoned with Maoist slogans. The grand hotels rattle with occasional Japanese and Albanian tourists.

Pedicab drivers, few as they are, seem hard put to find fares. Moreover, workers' pay is extremely low—well under thirty-five dollars a month, although rent, food, and medical care are even lower.

Yet the massive experiment appears to work. China already seems to have solved its food problem, the world's greatest (most basic Chinese problems are "the world's greatest"), and now it is perceptibly moving along the road to serious industrialization.

No one knows or really cares what the price of a car or tractor is; it will certainly be years before China enters competitive foreign-trade markets. The first job at hand is using Chinese machine products to benefit an enormous hinterland.

The financial system is primitive but curiously stable. More than half a century ago, history's most disastrous inflation wiped out the German economy; in October 1923, one U.S. penny could purchase 6,250,000 paper marks. Now, most nations are again frightened by an uncontrollable leap in prices. In 1973, Professor John Vaizey wrote in *International Currency Review:* "The current inflation is steadily accelerated toward the take-off point of hyper-inflation." One country spared this worry, because of its deliberate quest for autarky and its self-sufficient monetary system, is the People's Republic. A Peking magazine claims that "China is now a country free of domestic and foreign debts. . . . The People's Republic is completely free of the inflation and chaotic financial conditions characteristic of old China."

There are various reasons for this. China's only two foreign banks, the Chartered Bank of London and the Hong Kong and Shanghai Bank, have maintained offices in Shanghai ever since the Japanese occupation ended in 1945; each bank is represented by one Englishman plus Chinese assistants. There are eight foreign banks authorized by Peking to do business with China. None of these is American, as yet, but the six, including Pakistani and Swiss banks, without offices in Shanghai function mainly from New York, and all are confined to straightening out bureaucratic red tape involving letters of credit for purchases of Chinese exports.

The main financial institutions in China are the People's Bank, with branches all over the country, which takes savings deposits and issues checking accounts to co-operative shops; and the Bank of China, concerned with trade, which has branches in all main Chinese cities and in Hong Kong, London, and soon in Beirut. As nearly as I can figure (official statements to me were muddled in translation), the People's Bank gives interest rates of 2.7 per cent and 1.9 per cent on long-term and short-term deposits.

The yuan—China's equivalent of the dollar—has remained steady. Prices have mounted for goods involving foreigners, perhaps as a way to obtain more foreign currency. But the value of basic commodities is as constant as are the salaries for all Chinese.

Nobody is told how much money is in circulation or

what gold or foreign currency reserves amount to. There seems to be some link between the yuan and the value of East Europe's Comecon-bloc money. Britain's pound sterling depreciated against the yuan by 20 per cent during one recent period of eighteen months.

One of the three representatives I met with from the Chinese Academy of Science's Institute of Economics in Peking told me: "Unlike the West, our money mostly relies on commodities produced by our own national industries; and all our enterprises belong to the state. Currency in circulation is calculated against the amount of commodities produced to prevent imbalance. Therefore we don't have to issue notes to make up for financial deficits."

He explained that the state sold products abroad ignoring world prices and either taking a profit or deliberately absorbing a loss for reasons of over-all economic convenience.

Since China finished paying its debts of about $1.7 billion to the Soviet Union in 1965, it has owed nothing abroad except "deferred payments" for some short-term commercial loans, which usually carry interest charges of about 5 per cent.

The state owns everything except personal possessions like clothing and private peasant plots on communes, which amount to about 6 per cent of arable land. It does not rely on taxes to finance itself. Communes pay a collective agricultural tax of 6 per cent—which almost equals the output of private plots. Workers pay no income tax at all; their salaries are fixed by the state. Factories pay all profits to the government—minus production costs, including wages.

This system ignores the fluctuation of world-market economies and, it is true, limits China's vast population to very small amounts of cash. But unlike Russia, once a great breadbasket, which now has to resort to importing grain, China has become self-sufficient in food and is now able to give aid to developing countries. And again, one word that has faded from the national memory is "inflation."

Probably China's greatest internal preoccupation is the race between food supply and population growth. In a land of statistical secrecy it is hard to arrive at definitive conclusions. Yet there is every sign that despite their increasing number the Chinese people are being better fed. I talked with farmers on two communes, one near Peking and one in the province of Shensi, who both confirmed that, despite poor weather last year, China reaped a bumper crop.

Chen Chung, a bureau chief of Peking's Agriculture Ministry, said in late 1973: "We will have enough grain for all the population and also to continue storing reserves. The state has already stored 40 million tons, and our huge farming population has stored a large amount regionally." This is in keeping with Mao Tse-tung's instruction to stash food around the country as a security precaution in case of war and severed communications.

According to Chen, the annual rate of increase in grain output is between 4 and 5 per cent, whereas population growth is under 2 per cent. Observers question the latter figure, however, and think that it is at least 2 per cent.

Chen said that only 20 per cent of China's land is cultivated, but that "eventually the arable area can be doubled." He said that private peasant plots represent between 5 and 7 per cent of the acreage and produce an equivalent proportion of the harvest.

China's population is around 800 million and probably rising faster than Chen indicated. Nevertheless, at the commune of Shuang Chiao, I visited one family which seemed happy, reasonably fed, and pleased to show off the hens and the pair of pigs they owned; Chairman Mao has encouraged private pig-raising because "one pig is a small fertilizer factory."

Undoubtedly the biggest farm problems are lack of adequate agricultural machinery and chemical fertilizers. Recent movies of farms in Honan and Hopei confirm that an enormous amount of sowing, cultivating, and reaping is done by hand or by primitive tools such as mattocks. Fertilizer is heavily made up of animal or human manure, and in the Yenan area one sees many donkey-drawn carts containing large barrels of night soil.

China's fate is directly tied to that of its peasants, who make up 80 per cent of the population and on whom Maoism bases current ideology. The fact that agricultural output has overtaken the population growth rate makes it easier to conform to Chairman Mao's desire for approximate economic self-sufficiency.

Special emphasis is said to be placed on expansion of chemical-fertilizer plants, above all those based in rural areas, which now produce probably more than 60 per cent of China's total fertilizer output.

The revolutionary regime promptly collectivized all land, and in 1958 organized the communes, on which there are now some 750,000 work brigades. A commune is a large farm unit with thousands of members—something like the *agrogorod* which was tried in Russia after Stalin's death, unsuccessfully.

At first the central government in Peking thought that it could plan for and administer these numerous enterprises. However, it soon realized that it had to decentralize for efficiency—down to the level of the "production teams" which make up a "brigade." The brigades are charged annually as a unit, so that the individual farmers pay no direct income tax. A large portion of each peasant's communal profit is paid off in kind, especially in grain.

By 1971, China was producing annually about 17 million tons of invaluable chemical fertilizer but still importing 180 million dollars' worth. In an effort to develop even further its own fertilizer industry, China has been negotiating large contracts to purchase diammonium phosphate in the United States, as well as the material for the construction of three ammonia plants.

The national government is working all the time to produce more and more food, both for immediate consumption and for storage as a possible wartime reserve. The old-fashioned China of intermittent famines occasioned by alternating droughts and floods is no more. The Chinese peasant is still poor, but he is no longer hungry.

At the same time, the advance in highly specialized fields such as nuclear physics, missile engineering, and medicine—including ingenious and effective new uses of acupuncture and herbal cures—demonstrates that learning in China has been stifled neither by the superficially static code of Mao Tse-tung nor by the whirling experimentation of revolutionary practice. On the contrary, the Chinese have succeeded to a large extent in wiping out extensive venereal disease and in creating birth-control pills; they have also made notable advances in anesthesia and, in surgery, in the grafting of completely severed limbs.

There has, moreover, been a decided change in basic education since the Great Proletarian Cultural Revolution of 1966, which, like so many things in China nowadays, began in the mind of Chairman Mao, and which first manifested itself, violently, in the principal university centers.

It is now clear that the great goal of the shake-up, which caused large changes among party leaders and cadres and for a time threatened chaos, was to do away with any recrudescence of an established privileged learned class or mandarinate in which the educated civil servant is isolated from what Maoism calls "popular reality."

The resulting upheaval in educational methods is obviously related to the new attack on Confucianism, which had been fixed doctrinal ideology for China's successive dynasties to the extent that a man well versed in its tenets could claim, and get, a good job. Confucius's most famous pupil, Mencius, went so far as to write that "gentlemen are there to rule the people, the people to feed the gentle-men."

There is now a kind of accelerated and shortened teach-ing system in which, at the end of secondary school, every student is sent into a factory or to a communal farm. Be-fore being allowed to go on to higher studies, he must be recommended by the masses.

This means that there are vast numbers of Chinese whose learning stops at the secondary-school level. But they have their place in society; for example, the "barefoot doctors" or, in Inner Mongolia, the "horseback doctors," who give primitive first aid to local patients.

Moreover, there are many opportunities for self-improve-ment through the equivalent of correspondence courses. For example, Peking Radio gives regular English lessons, and Shanghai Radio offers courses in English, French, and Japanese.

Because of the interval on farms or in factories, students are older than before, generally from twenty to twenty-six, when they matriculate.

In 1971, regular college curricula were cut from five to three years and many courses were dropped as "super-fluous," to make more time to integrate students "into our existing society," as the head of a university in Huhehot, Inner Mongolia, explained to me.

Even faculty members are forced to spend some time teaching in rural areas or working in factories, some of them small enough to be run by the universities themselves. The professors thereby spread learning among the people and themselves keep in touch with the needs of the masses.

It is too early to measure the ultimate value of this novel educational approach to Chinese society as a whole. But the logic behind it is understandable in a land that has such a long tradition of division between classes, where the white-collar class has disdained to associate with the blue-collar proletariat once it attained privilege, through inheritance or through a college degree and successful civil-service examinations.

There can be no doubt that the new educational system furthers the egalitarian aims of the People's Republic and continues to churn its evolving society, minimizing the possibility that a permanent bureaucracy can ever emerge at the top. The only question remaining to be answered is how costly this experiment might turn out to be in terms of that danger Alexander Pope discerned in "a little learning."

Before the Maoist revolution, the role of Chinese women was markedly inferior. Confucius more or less set the pattern when he wrote that "only women and low-class men are hard to keep. If allowed to approach you, they show no respect; if kept at a distance, they complain." Lu Hsun commented: "This is the complaint of most male supremacists today. It is the affliction of most women too."

Women were traditionally regarded as breeders and second class, although there have been outstanding exceptions, including Sung dynasty poetesses, a few imperial wives and concubines who greatly influenced policy, and even that ghastly figure the tyrannical dowager empress who died in 1908. Those famous sisters Mrs. Sun Yat-sen and Mrs. Chiang Kai-shek each wielded great influence during her husband's period of power.

In the outmoded social system prevailing into this century, with China's enormous pockets of poverty and famine, women and girls were habitually disadvantaged. Daughters of peasants were often sold into slavery or concubinage, and girl babies were frequently left to die from exposure.

To protect their health and avoid the problems of overpopulation imposed by male chauvinists who sometimes fortified themselves with aphrodisiacs like powdered rhinoceros horn, Chinese women began to practice peasant forms of birth control, such as devouring tadpoles.

One massive problem of the Maoist revolution was how

to liberate the women or, in terms of politics and economics, how to achieve a sexless as well as a classless society. The Maoists have come a long way in this but there
is still a long way for them to go.

Women wear the same egalitarian costume as men.
Just as class distinction between the gaudy clothing of the
rich and the tattered clothing of the poor has been essentially eliminated, so has the basic contrast in costume of
men and women. Both wear a kind of baggy pajama suit
or cotton dungarees that tend to disguise differences in
human architecture.

Men and women do much the same kind of work. You
can pass fields during harvest time and see the two sexes
participating equally. In some industrial processes, of
course, there are differences. I have seen textile and carpet
factories where more women than men tended machines
and looms, and also construction projects where more men
than women did the heavy labor.

The vice-chairman of Shanghai's principal shipyard told
me that women workers were used for welding, lathe-
turning, truck-driving, and crane-operating, and that
women were allowed to sail on coastal ships but not to
crew on ocean-going vessels.

Women have benefited enormously from a new and
pervasive drive for family planning. When Allen Dulles
headed the C.I.A., he foolishly speculated that China was
planning to use its enormous population as a political
weapon by exporting increasing numbers of Chinese to
establish racial colonies the world over. This is clearly not
the case. The state is serious about birth control. Pills and
other types of contraceptives are distributed free. Chinese
women have told me that they universally support this
government program.

But genuine political equality of the sexes has yet to be
achieved in People's China. Not one of the five vice-chairmen of the Communist party is a woman. On the twenty-

one-member Politburo, there is only one woman; there is one among three alternate Politburo members, and none on the six-member standing committee. Only 12.9 per cent of the delegates who attended last year's Tenth Party Congress were women.

It is officially stated that "in new China equal pay is given for equal work, as well as special protection for women workers." Women receive free pre- and post-natal care and maternity leave with pay. The revolutionary marriage law stipulates free choice of partner. This is an earth-shaking change in most of China. Indeed, Pasang, vice-chairwoman of the Tibetan Revolutionary Committee, was a slave until she was eighteen.

Last year the *People's Daily* warned that "no factory should discriminate against women," implying that, despite the official "equal pay for equal work," this was not always the case. The same editorial urged that women be given "a better understanding of the political situation."

Some of the other social questions are less openly discussed than women's lib. For instance, when I asked Chu Mu-chih, a member of the Communist Party Central Committee and head of Hsinhua, the New China News Agency, how crime was reported in the press, he replied: "Generally we don't report such things because they are not in the mainstream of life. . . . We let the people know about such cases by other methods. In our country, if there is a serious criminal case, it is not just a police matter. The masses take part in investigating it. A court, when making judgment, explains its views to the people and they explain their reactions. We do not have a jury system. In major cases, the public sometimes puts out public notices."

Chu said that although treason, murder, "serious arson, and serious rape" were punishable by death, "our system is to kill as little as possible. We cannot yet do away with capital punishment. Generally executions are by shooting.

But there are two kinds of treatment: one is immediate execution because the people are disgusted by a crime; the other is sentencing to death but postponement of execution for one or two years. If the criminal acts well and reforms, sentence is remitted."

In northern Shensi province, I asked Tu Chin-chang, of the Yenan Revolutionary Committee, if there was a criminal problem. He said there "are some thieves," and these are dealt with by the Public Security Bureau (P.S.B.), a kind of national police force. Thieves are released "after criticism and education," but he wouldn't indicate how long that process took. "Class enemies or those who refuse to recant" are sent to jail; but these were "rare."

He said that in his area the courts consisted of judges, elected by the people, together with what is "like a jury" of three or four persons. The judge does the sentencing. Murderers are bound and forced to listen to public denunciations and then taken to a distant place and shot. He would not say how large a firing squad was, but added that "it takes only one man with a gun to kill."

As far as I can ascertain, there is no statute book or criminal code available in any foreign language, and I am not at all certain that such a document exists in Chinese. Ma Yü-chen, deputy director of information for the Foreign Ministry, told me that all laws are new and revolutionary, although some minor statutes were "based on a study of foreign codes."

When I asked whether there had ever been any cases of corruption among high officials, he said there had been one, apparently just below the vice-ministerial level, and that the offender was "tried by a people's court, convicted, and shot."

The Ministry of Justice and the Public Procuratorship initially set up by the People's Republic were both abolished in the 1960's. There are no longer any career judges.

Law is essentially enforced by the Communist party, which administers neighborhood revolutionary committees, who keep a sharp eye out for offenders.

There seems to be a problem with youngsters rebelling against being sent to rural areas for a few years after finishing high school. Some sneak illegally back to cities, where, since they are without the registration cards that entitle them to purchase clothing, rice, and oil, they often turn to stealing.

This does not appear to be a serious difficulty, however. The Public Security Bureau, under the Minister of Public Security, handles transgressions beyond the reach of the local revolutionary committee and runs the labor reform camps.

Unquestionably, there is less crime in People's China than in most countries. Violators are generally punished by party administrative fiat. Licentiousness and bureaucratic favoritism are roughly dealt with.

One hears little nowadays about the public "trials" mentioned by Tu Chin-chang, and nothing about public executions before large crowds encouraged to revile the bodies.

In the unusual instance of a death sentence that is not deferred, the firing squad is made up of P.S.B. members. P.S.B. units themselves have been separated from the regular People's Liberation Army, which is disengaging itself increasingly from civil affairs.

As in all Communist countries, there is internal censorship of the press; the media are expected to put forth the government's viewpoint only. Objectivity, in the Western sense, or reportorial initiative, is banned. China differs in this from other Marxist lands only in the totality of its propaganda effort, which makes even Russia seem relatively open. News is deliberately kept from the inquiring foreigner, and even approved, official papers cannot be bought at kiosks by those visitors who can read Chinese. A great deal of information of the most important sort is either held up indefinitely or delayed for a long time before publication: for example, "delicate news" like the alleged assassination plot against Mao by Lin Piao and then Lin's death in the crash of his fleeing hijacked airplane; and even the recent Middle East war, the gravity of which was played down in the Chinese press for days.

Indeed, an American journalist must travel through the looking glass to understand the role of the press and other media in the People's Republic, where it is not so much a question of giving the people light so they can find their own way, or of publishing all the news that's fit to print, as of directing the people along a way to find the light already selected for them, or printing the news that already fits.

Contemporary editors refer one to the remarks of Mao Tse-tung himself in his discussion many years ago with the staff of the *Shansi-Suiyuan Daily:* "The role and power of the newspapers consists in their ability to bring the party program, the party line, the party's general and specific policies, its tasks and methods of work before the masses in the quickest and most extensive way. . . . Your job is to educate the masses, to enable the masses to know their own interests, their own tasks and the party's general and specific policies."

Keeping to this guideline, the Chinese press and radio do not even attempt to give either objective or complete pictures of the world's news; and television is limited in both scope and availability. The only objective and relatively complete information is distributed in *Reference News,* a "private bulletin" put out by Hsinhua.

According to Chu Mu-chih, *Reference News* is not published in any papers, although it has an enormous circulation among selected officials, students, workers, commune leaders, and party members. "Nearly seven million copies are distributed every day, and perhaps as many as ten persons read each copy," he told me.

This "private" report contains foreign news, both favorable and unfavorable to Maoism, which may be of

interest to China, and makes no editorial comment itself
—"so that our readers," said Chu, "can better judge events
themselves." This, he claimed, proved China's journalistic
objectivity, adding that "Western journalism pretends to
be objective but isn't."

Chu became a newspaperman in Nanking during the
Japanese war and then joined the Communist underground. He said that foreign broadcasts to China were not
jammed, but admitted that "apart from our people in
Hsinhua, few others listen to them." "They aren't interested," he explained. "Anyway, we never check up on
this." I am under the impression that such broadcasts
would be difficult to pick up on many Chinese radios; also,
that the habit of listening to them might well close paths
to success.

The Hsinhua chief explained that the two kinds of wall
posters, which figured so much during the Cultural Revolution, have the "same basic function" as the press.
"Large-character" posters were put up by any individuals
who so desired. Wang Hung-wen, new young Politburo
member and probably number-three hierarch in the party,
recommends their extensive use so "the masses . . . air
their views freely." "Small-character" posters are edited
like miniature newspapers.

I was told that there is "no censorship" because everything reflects the party line but that "a journalist writing
his own comments consults experts first." I personally en-
countered no censorship of the columns I transmitted
abroad to *The New York Times,* although I suspect that
any sharply hostile observations would not have greatly
facilitated my stay.

Technically, most presses and communications equipment are now made in China, but some material, especially
teletypes, is imported from West Germany. Most news-
print is Chinese, although some has to be brought in from
Sweden.

The largest and most important paper in China is the

Peking *People's Daily,* with a circulation of 3.5 million—
1.4 million in the capital and 2.1 million in eleven other
cities, which print some hours later from facsimile trans-
missions of air-shipped mats.

Wen Huei Bo, the larger of Shanghai's papers, according to its editors, has a circulation of 900,000—not much
for the biggest city on the Eurasian land mass. Like the
other journals in China, it consists of only four pages. In
the midst of the Middle East war, the main item on the
front page was an "editorial" about a new Chinese opera.

The impact of Mao's revolution is still hard to assess.
Yet Napoleon is credited with having said that China is a
sleeping giant and when it awakes the world will tremble.
The Chinese giant has awakened from its long, long
slumber, although, despite Soviet pretensions to anxiety,
there seems no reason for the world's trembling. In fact,
one is inclined to wonder if China did not wake up too
late.

As for the fascinating, if often puzzling, Maoist philosophy, I simply question whether in this era of quantum
jumps, when most lands must run hard to stay in the
same place, China can achieve its aims quickly enough and
on a sufficiently massive scale to keep up with the great
powers. The gap between the earth's rich and poor
widens. China has closed that gap internally; can it do so
in terms of the outside world?

While many underdeveloped countries have come a
long way from where they were a mere generation ago,
they have slipped even farther back in relation to major
industrial societies. They have become actually richer but
relatively poorer.

The only outstanding modern exceptions to this rule are
nations that took off with the help of foreign investments.
India—not yet out of the swamp—has absorbed billions in
foreign aid. Even the Soviet Union was bolstered from

abroad in its early days and has now turned back again
in a search for technological help. Meanwhile, Maoism's
do-it-yourself revolution has managed to build a strong
military establishment, even to enter the thermonuclear
age, and to develop an industrial infrastructure.

The autarkic tradition is familiar to China, whose emperor told the eighteenth-century British envoy Lord
Macartney: "Our celestial empire possesses all things in
prolific abundance. . . . There is therefore no need to
import the manufactures of outside barbarians." But one
wonders if the People's Republic can maintain these enormous undertakings at a sufficiently rapid pace to gain in
relative international terms. I remember in 1950 talking to
an important Russian, who, discussing Chinese needs,
said: "Russia alone cannot handle the problem. It is a
thirty-year task for America and Russia together."

This implication is precisely what Peking objects to
nowadays—that it should be overshadowed by the two
superpowers. The fact is that it is also being overtaken by
the nonsuperpowers, including West Germany and Japan.
Nevertheless, the People's Republic has accomplished a
great deal, although anyone brought up under ethical traditions by which the higher value is placed on individual
liberty would hate living there. As in all revolutions, the
Chinese upheaval saw much brutality and killing. China is
large and the statistics are formidable. But it must be re-
membered that there are hundreds of millions of survivors
who are doing better than their parents could have imag-
ined. They have shelter, clothes, food, jobs, and most of
them are literate. What they do not have is freedom of
choice, but I venture to say that no clamorous majority
demands it. The traditions of imperial, Confucianist China
bred a different kind of man from what English common
law or the American frontier did.

Mao Tse-tung's thought "answers" all current problems.
It makes good crops, raises coal production, stimulates

painters, improves ping-pong. Even though the Little Red Book of Chairman Mao's thoughts is less in evidence than it was just four years ago, it is still a veritable panacea, an atheistic Koran.

At this stage, Maoism is not dynamic or expansionist; it is committed to self-reliance, and so avoids contemporary blights like fuel shortages. It wants to hold what it has, not to take what belongs to others. And, in line with this autarkic philosophy, it does not seek help from abroad.

Only an ideologue well versed in Marxism can predict what course Maoism will follow once Mao is dead. After all, who could have forecast when Lenin died that Stalin would elbow aside the brilliant Trotsky and Bukharin and succeed him, clamping down a leaden dictatorship far transcending even Lenin's in its ruthlessness and authoritarianism? With this in mind, I once asked Djilas, erstwhile number-two man in Yugoslavia and today a heretic in his own heretical land, in disgrace because of his personal split with Tito's version of Marxist doctrine, how he viewed Maoist China.

"Mao was treated as a godlike figure, like Stalin," he replied. "But there were major differences. Mao was the first Marxist to say that the classless society must be educated and developed in a period of centuries, not decades. . . . And Mao has understood that what has come about in Russia now is the development of a new privileged class. He is trying to prevent the same thing from happening in China; but he will succeed only during his own lifetime, as long as he lives. After he dies everything will change."

3

Karl Marx and Confucian Confusion

It is an especially puzzling paradox that although Stalin's picture is still featured in public squares in China (along with Marx, Engels, Lenin, and—in top position, bigger and apart—Chairman Mao), he was really Mao's first great Russian adversary. He strongly supported Chiang Kai-shek until the Generalissimo's political collapse. It was Stalin who signed the Yalta accord, giving Chiang a favored position over the Chinese Communists; Stalin who ordered his ambassador to proceed southward as far as Canton with Chiang's defeated troops, until they took off across the water for Taiwan—no other country did as much.

The first Chinese revolution, comparable to that of Kerensky in Russia, ended with the abdication of the imperial dynasty in 1912 and the establishment of a republic that was grudgingly acknowledged by the last czar. U.S. Ambassador Curtis Guild was able to report from St. Petersburg, as his successor might just as well report from Moscow today: "The Minister of Foreign Affairs frankly states that Russia does not wish to see a strong military power in China."

Nevertheless, after the Bolshevik revolution, the policy of the newly created Soviet Union toward China became a domestic issue in the struggle between Stalin and Trotsky to succeed Lenin. Trotsky, as people's commissar for foreign affairs, knew at least something about China, and had even approached the Chinese Minister, Liu Ching-jen, about liquidating the old "unequal treaty" arrangements that had given Chinese domains to Russia.

However, during these early Soviet years, in reaction

to Trotsky's more orthodox policy, Stalin became more and more deeply attached to the ideas of Chinese President Sun Yat-sen and then to those of his successor Chiang. As the American Sinologue John Paton Davies, Jr., wrote in *Dragon by the Tail*: "Trotsky was quite right in accusing Stalin of being hoodwinked by Chiang and binding the miserable Chinese Communists to the Kuomintang Chariot."

But Sun had sent the young Chiang to Moscow in 1923 as head of a republican delegation. Two years later, just before his death, Sun left a political testament to his government expressing "the hope that the day is approaching when the Soviet Union will greet in a free and strong China its friend and ally, and that the two states will proceed hand in hand as allies in the great fight for the emancipation of the whole world." If Stalin was "hoodwinked" by Chiang, Sun was absolutely deluded by Stalin.

The basic issue in the Stalin-Trotsky argument over China policy was whether the Chinese Communists, then a small faction, should be urged to collaborate with Chiang's Kuomintang or encouraged to pursue an independent line. Stalin insisted on the former, and won. Meanwhile, Chiang had become the powerful commandant of the Whampoa Military Academy, created by Kuomintang-Soviet collaboration as a military-political school for revolutionists. Mikhail Borodin was sent to Canton, stronghold of the Kuomintang, as Moscow's agent to strengthen the Chinese faction Stalin had determined to sponsor.

The Canton movement dissolved, and Borodin eventually returned to Russia, disillusioned and complaining: "When the next Chinese general comes to Moscow and shouts: 'Hail to the World Revolution!' better send at once for the G.P.U."

Nevertheless, although Chiang turned on those Chinese Communists who had collaborated warily with him in Shanghai, and smashed them by a sudden coup in 1927, he and his Kuomintang remained Stalin's chosen instruments for unifying China. Moscow continued to send them both advisers and weapons and to condemn the Russian Communists who wished to break with this dubious policy.

Last year, the diary of a Soviet adviser in China during the 1942–1945 period was published in Moscow. This quoted Mao as saying (July 29, 1942): "Stalin does not and cannot know China. And yet he presumes to judge everything. All his so-called theories on our revolution are the blabberings of a fool." That October, according to the diarist, Pavel Vladimirov, Mao shouted at some of his opponents: "You Muscovites, even if Stalin farts you are ready to admire the smell." And yet, despite the long history of mistrust between the two famous Communist leaders, Stalin's face still features in orthodox public displays in Maoist China.

It was only when Mao and his military forces finally smashed Chiang and expelled him from the Asian continent that Stalin recognized the strength of Chinese Communism. The potential dynamic power of this little-known (at least to him) movement on Russia's eastern flank, and its unorthodox and deviationist tendencies, began to worry him in earnest.

Stalin did resolve to back up his change in policy, dictated by events, by sending aid, technicians, and material to the new revolutionary China. This and admiration for his autocratic methods were what earned him a place in Mao's gallery of honored heroes.

It is convenient for Maoism to erase the historical chapter portraying Stalin's opposition to China's struggling Communist party, and to blame Khrushchev, who de-Stalinized Russia, and Brezhnev, who came later, for all that really stems from the original long-term Stalinist policy.

In contemporary China, Maoism is both political doctrine and ideology, almost religion. The new party

constitution specifically defines "Marxism–Leninism–Mao
Tse-tung thought as the theoretical basis guiding its think-
ing." A plenum agreed: "Mao Tse-tung thought should
be taken as the guide for action."

Chairman Mao has written several works, some yet to
be published. His mottoes, strategy, policy guidelines,
dogma are familiar to most Chinese. He is quoted on a
huge placard at airports: "Go all out and aim high." In
the vast network of tunneled air-raid shelters: "Dig deep."
In peasant communes: "Store grain."

His enormous photograph is widely displayed and on a
larger scale than those of Marx, Engels, Lenin, and Stalin.
In the first Central Committee headquarters, built outside
Yenan in 1942, where Mao ran meetings, played ping-
pong and chess with delegates, and elaborated theory, his
picture now dwarfs those of all the other heroes of socialism.

Mao himself has acknowledged that there is political use
in such a personality cult. He told the late Edgar Snow
that Khrushchev probably fell because he had no personality cult. As Peyrefitte perceptively points out, Maoism is
not just a theory, but essentially a method; it has to be
lived. It also has to be related to the ancient Chinese
thought patterns, above all to yin and yang, the positive
and negative that make up any whole. Mao once said
when retreating from a town: "One wins Yenan by losing
Yenan." His wife, the influential Chiang Ching, says:
"Good" is the "thought" of Chairman Mao and those in-
spired by it; "evil" is everything else.

The philosophical import of Mao's thoughts has not yet
been measured. His strategic teachings have had major
importance. His political doctrine of a continuing revolution may prove as significant, over the decades, as his
military doctrine of revolutionary warfare.

But there is another aspect of Maoism which the West
would call religious. Mao himself is not devout and, as a

youth, sided with his irreligious father against his Buddhist mother, whom he otherwise vastly preferred.

All the old faiths are rarely practiced in China now, even Confucianism, which was more a practical philosophy than a creed. Christianity, Buddhism, Islam are virtually gone. There is not one lama left in Buddhistic Inner Mongolia, according to officials there. Nevertheless, Marxism, Chinese-style, has become a faith, and Mao Tse-tung is its prophet.

One is shown, like stations of the cross, the quarters in and around cave-rimmed Yenan where Mao dwelt during the revolution's heroic days. In terms of "protracted warfare," Yenan is the Valley Forge of Maoist China.

Mao has demonstrated both that he is an earthy, commonsensical man and that he is audacious in the revolutionary sense of Danton. "Don't be afraid to make trouble," he argues. "Confusion and trouble are always noteworthy." And he once exuberantly proclaimed that "it will be intolerable if after several decades we are not the greatest nation on earth."

In chilly, gray-green, mountainous Yenan, with its generations-old, hollowed-out dwellings where a seventh-century Tang-dynasty pagoda still leans peacefully from a hill, one is reminded of the eternal China from which Maoism stemmed. In the first century B.C., the Emperor Wu Ti advocated state ownership to protect the destitute. In A.D. 9, the Emperor Wang Mang ordered great land reforms. In the eleventh century, Chancellor Wang An-shih instructed the state to take over the management of commerce, industry, and agriculture.

Contemporary Chinese concepts are thus related to the distant past. But, apart from this eminently practical heritage, from which Maoism is historically derived, there is its religious aspect. Jean-François Billeter, a French scholar, points out that Confucianism "was above all a moral system and a political ideology, that of the scholar-official class." This is perhaps why Confucius is now being criticized as "reactionary." As Billeter writes, Confucianism was "an ideology of the ruling class."

In China, traditional theology was less preoccupied with metaphysics than in the Occident. The logic practiced seems strange to a Westerner. There is less interest in quests for abstract truth than in practical application of wisdom. This, I believe, is the kernel of Maoist thought.

Today, Mao is, in effect, chairman of the board of that great enterprise called "China." He is semiretired now, but still makes all the major policy decisions.

Chairman Mao, as he is always respectfully called, is probably one of this century's best Chinese poets. He is strong and lusty; he has had four wives and at least six children. His first wife, his sister, and two brothers died violently during the civil war, and one of his sons was killed in the Korean conflict.

His will power and ambition are formidable. He told a French group that, yes, Robespierre was a great revolutionary but that he was more impressed by Napoleon. "Never be associated with failure . . ." he warned a comrade years ago. "Any person who receives our support and does not fulfill his part of the bargain must become the target for frontal attack of pitiless ferocity."

Mao is as wily as he is ruthless. In July 1945, he gave his deliberately fostered personality cult a boost by writing in an anonymous article that the Chinese people wanted to follow "Mao Tse-tung's way."

Machiavelli observed that "the first impression that one gets of a ruler and of his brains is from seeing the men he has about him." One knows from talking with Mao's right hand, Chou, that Mao is remarkable, just as one would have known it from talking to former lieutenants, now all dead or—in the Orwellian sense—"unpersons," who once seemed to outrank and outshine Chou.

Mao always imposed his will upon himself, and after

that upon others. As a youth, he built up his physique to a point where he became famous for his endurance. He earned his meals by doing itinerant farm work in his native Hunan, and at the same time toughened his stomach by a Spartan diet.

He conceived and pushed through, against overwhelming odds, the famous Long March of 1934. He is like Stalin in his personal regime as well as its effect on his followers. Thus, although most Chinese prefer to leave work early and rise early, China's top men now work late and rise late in keeping with Mao's own habits.

Mao was a modest schoolteacher for a long time, and attained more knowledge reading late by candlelight than at a university. His tastes have always been simple: plain food, chess, ping-pong. His speeches and pronouncements are studded with homely phrases like "bean-curd tiger," "sparrow warfare," "paper tiger," "running dogs."

If he is just as ambitious as Stalin, whose self-advertising he emulates (although there has recently been a slight decline in public adulation), he is infinitely more patient: he thinks of revolutionary success in terms of decades or even generations. He has not created a new Marxist kind of thought, but in both politics and war he has profoundly adjusted some aspects of Marxism to Chinese circumstances.

His monumentally important decision to base the revolution on China's peasantry rather than on its urban workers was an idea debated and discarded by the Comintern in Lenin's day. And, although his traditional military doctrine is a bad digestion of Clausewitz via Lenin, he brilliantly adapted the 2,500-year-old strategies of Sun Tzu to contemporary guerrilla warfare. Moreover, he proved himself a partisan hero.

He has often produced an amalgam of others' ideas rather than a synthesis; for example, his "continuing (national) revolution" version of Trotsky's "permanent (global) revolution." And, while keeping the army in discipline, he has made it a school for mass ideological transformation.

These days Mao is sinking gradually. He is in his capital no more than four months a year. His portrait is everywhere, but his real face is to be seen infrequently. In Peking, he lives in the southwest corner of the Forbidden City enclave, among his books. He is in touch often, but for short stretches now, with such lieutenants as Chou, who can reach him quickly through the capital's famous network of underground tunnels.

Mao has set the stamp of his intellect and personality on modern China just as Lenin set the stamp of his intellect and personality on modern Russia. In one poem Mao wrote: "For heroes, now is the time." But "now" it is evident the Chairman is starting physically to fail. Resolute as he is, Mao has one ineluctable weakness: he is mortal.

This is a weakness shared by Chou. I know of no partnership, no collaboration (in both senses of the word) in history like theirs. They have worked hand in hand for more than two generations reshaping the ideological, political, military, and administrative apparatus of the world's largest country.

If Mao holds a position in China equivalent to that of a corporate chairman of the board, Chou can be called the managing director. He applies on a practical basis the revolutionary theorems worked out by Mao and the top leadership. He has had quite as long a personal relationship to China's Communist revolution as Mao has. Forty-one years ago he was named political commissar for the Red Army, now the People's Liberation Army, during a neap tide when Mao had begun to lose authority.

But Chou is not a music maker, a dreamer of dreams, like Mao; he is more the traditional executive. In recent years, and especially since the purge and death of Lin in 1971, he has stressed again and again that he has no interest in succeeding to power, only in applying that power

which is his through his association with another. There
is no "Chouism" in People's China, only Maoism.

Chou will go down with Mao. They are bracketed together by age, by experience, and by division of assign-
ments. Their relationship has been a triumph over all the
differences between them: Mao is of peasant origin, Chou
a minor mandarin; Mao's allegiance is to the continental
isolationism of a China that viewed foreign traditions as
"barbarian," whereas Chou was one of the animators of
the Chinese Communist party's French section and has
always been as much concerned with foreign as with internal policy. Chou was political commissar of Chiang
Kai-shek's Whampoa Military Academy in 1925. When
an uneasy Kuomintang-Communist alliance was fighting
Japan, Chou was Mao's man at Chiang's headquarters. He
can look back on both the Paris Left Bank and international gatherings in Chungking.

If Chou is not the dynamist to launch a new historic
wave, he can certainly recognize such a wave before it has
even become a ripple. "Revolution," he says, "is the main
trend of the world today." The original facets, the new
impetus, were supplied primarily by Mao. Chou was the
supreme executor; and so he remains.

Today, the revolution's right-hand man is smaller,
frailer, more tired-looking than he looks in his photo-
graphs. In repose, his face is tough—and fatigued. His war
wounds show on his body (above all, on his right arm)
and his soul scars show on his visage. He has several times
indicated that he has no intention of undertaking any more
foreign travel.

Perhaps, looking back on his own life, he can take the
most pride in his increasing emphasis on China's internal
revolutionary problems rather than on its external global
role. "A revolution is just like a human being," he says.
"It can be regenerated by continuous changes in metabo-
lism."

In light of his own international position, it is worth

stressing his conclusion: "For us, ourselves, the most important thing is to handle China's affairs well. For a country like China, with so large a population, it will take us several decades to develop our economy. That won't be done during the twentieth century. We will need millions of trained successors to carry on this program."

But will those "trained successors" be allowed to proceed without foreign interference, above all from Moscow? And who are those "trained successors"? And what course will they proceed along? These are the greatest questions in revolutionary China now.

The ideology forged by Maoism during its quarter century of authoritarian control over People's China has shuttled leftward and rightward. Figures like Liu Shao-chi or Lin Piao have risen to prominence and then plummeted into ignominy. The stratagem of enlisting support from the "petty bourgeoisie" and "national bourgeoisie" to overthrow a corrupt governing system and oust local war lords was swiftly forgotten when Communist authority became established and even the vestigial remnants of nonpeasant and nonworker classes could be discarded.

Likewise, the tolerance of religion—always discouraged and only reluctantly accepted—was abandoned. The massive but loosely organized Taoist and Buddhist structures, together with their priesthoods, were banned in fact, if not in theory. There were once almost 50 million practicing Moslems in China, but they have been squeezed down into a handful of living archaeological shards. China's ancient Jewish colony had been absorbed into the Sinic bloodstream long before the twentieth-century upheavals. Christianity was never a major influence on the national culture, even though both Chiang Kai-shek and his American-educated wife are Methodists. And where necessary, as in autonomous Inner Mongolia and Tibet, the tough fabric of lamaist Buddhism, a very durable and special sect, was simply wiped out, along with its clergy.

No differentiation was made between deist and purely philosophical beliefs that were distinct from Marxism, as interpreted in Peking. Confucius himself, the most famous of ancient Chinese thinkers, was officially and emphatically denounced in 1973. Even Plato was condemned late that year, for inspiring the "reactionary characteristics" of that archconspirator and sudden "unperson" Lin Piao.

The poor Athenian genius was also held responsible for some of the ideas of Liu Shao-chi, another "unperson," who had, in fact, been Lin Piao's enemy. It is hard to believe that Platonism was described in the *People's Daily* as "a pool of dead water reeking with the stink of the bourgeoisie." But then, both Liu and Lin are nowadays condemned as Russian sympathizers although they fought each other on that particular issue before they were, one after the other, destroyed by the Maoist machine.

In all this rewriting, or reattribution, of history, Confucius, of course, as the most Chinese of classical thinkers, is the most important symbol. As he is by far the best-known ancient Chinese sage, and the most respected in the international sense, it comes as a surprise to foreigners that he should be the center of a raging and crucial political storm. The external aspects of the battle over Confucius focus on Russian policy. Moscow is accused of using Confucianism to encourage anti-Mao and "bourgeois" reactionaries. As evidence, party leaders cite an article on Confucius in the last Great Soviet Encyclopedia and articles on him in the March and June 1973 issues of the Russian magazine *Questions of History.*

In China itself, Confucianism is regarded as a symbol of conservative forces still favoring the theories of Liu and Lin. No one claims Liu and Lin were actually coconspirators, just that their aims were similar—to oust Mao and to set China along a vehemently retrogressive path. It is furthermore alleged that their ideas are still endorsed by some elements in the ruling Communist party, and that this is why the Kremlin is pushing Confucius for everything he is worth.

Confucius, it is argued, was a reactionary even in his own day and was opposed by a "legalist" faction headed by Hsao Cheng-mao, whom Confucius, who happened to be minister of justice in his native state of Lu, then executed. Ever since, one is told, "Confucianist" has been a relatively right-wing term, and "legalist" a relatively left-wing one.

Shen Kuo-hsiang, editor of Shanghai's larger daily, assembled his chief ideologists to brief me on the Confucius question. Shen described Confucius as "a spokesman of the declining slave-owning system of the fifth century B.C. at a time when it was being replaced by the relatively more progressive landlord system. Confucius spent his entire life propagating reactionary views."

Official publications all condemn the ancient sage, throwing in Liu, Lin, Moscow, and Mencius. A first-dynasty emperor is extolled merely because he burned Confucian books and buried some Confucian scholars alive. Lin, on the other hand, took to criticizing this emperor, some say to blacken Mao.

Nobody pretends that anyone is going to be buried alive or that any books are going to be burned as a result of the present furor. Anti-Confucianism is, after all, a very old phenomenon among Chinese progressives. The "May 4" political movement of 1919, which led to formation of the Chinese Communist party two years later, is said to have started out with attacks on Confucius. Mao himself, one is told, denounced him before 1919, and then again, more elaborately, in 1927, 1939, 1940, and after 1949.

"Liu Shao-chi, our greatest capitalist-roader," Shen told me, "continually propagated Confucianism and actually wrote a book frequently quoting him. Lin Piao didn't write a book but often cited Confucius in speeches. Therefore when criticizing Liu and Lin, we must criticize Confucius. We are aware that future revisionists and bourgeois agents in our party will also make use of Confucius. This is a matter of political philosophy, not religion."

I asked if the new anti-Confucius drive might not be the beginning of the end of some Chinese leader or even the beginning of the downgrading of the dead Stalin, who, though he often disagreed with Maoist tenets, is still regarded as the equal of Marx and Lenin. "We still think of Stalin as a great Marxist," Shen said.

The fact is that many foreign scholars have also labeled Confucius reactionary. Stuart Schram, an American expert on Russian and Chinese Communism, calls "the Confucian view of politics . . . hierarchical and largely undemocratic." Chiang Kai-shek, in contrast, wrote in *China's Destiny* in 1943 that the last word on nearly everything had been said by Confucius.

In the curiously convoluted language of Chinese Communism, the teachings, the very name of Confucius, have a vastly important symbolic meaning. As Shen says: "We believe that bourgeois agents within our party will use Confucianism against our ideology, and therefore we will go on criticizing him. In this way, we root out remnants of the exploiting classes. You must realize socialism is a long, protracted stage of development and therefore the ideological struggle will be long and protracted. So will the criticism of Confucius."

Mixed with the insistence that Maoism is the only true faith for China is an insistence that the dominant Han species must and will prevail, and that minority races should be seen and cared for like tenants of a museum or a zoo. I have not had a chance to see how this is applied to the enormous but forbidden areas of Sinkiang (Chinese Turkestan) or Tibet, but I did see for myself the consequences of this insistence in Inner Mongolia, where the Mongol minority, although cherished in cotton wool, is being drowned in a flood of Hans.

This fact has particular importance in terms of the

Sino-Soviet confrontation. In the whole history of interaction between China and Russia, no area has been more
catalytic than the nebulous plateau of Mongolia, from
which emerged the conquerors of both the Russian and
the Chinese empires, as well as of much of the rest of
Asia and Europe. Therefore, Mongolia (including the
Soviet district of Buryat Mongolia, the Soviet satellite of
Outer Mongolia, and the Chinese autonomous province
of Inner Mongolia) has played a special and immensely
significant historical role. In a sense, it was the Mongols
who, once they had been constricted to their native steppes,
introduced the Russians and the Chinese to each other.

In 1570, a Chinese statesman named Wan Chun-hu
memorialized the Emperor, Lung Ching, suggesting that
the way to handle the menace of the warlike Mongolians
to the north was to convert them to Buddhism.

The Mongols had already been exposed to Buddhism,
even before their great king, Kubla Khan, overran China
and established the Yuan dynasty, which ruled a great
Chinese empire for a short while. During this period,
lamas from the vast prairie land went to study in distant
Tibet, but most Mongols preferred their own heathen
shaman rites.

Wan, fearing the fierce Mongol cavalry, counseled Emperor Lung: "Buddhism forbids bloodshed, prescribes
confession, recommends a virtuous life; for this reason we
should do our utmost to diffuse that faith among the
nomads."

Lung agreed, and the Ming and succeeding Ching emperors all propagated the Buddhist ideology throughout
Inner Mongolia, just as Mao has propagated Communist
ideology since he took control there in 1947.

Lamaism became the state religion of Mongolia; each
family was forced to contribute a son to the monasteries,
and potential warriors were thus turned into celibate
monks. The population naturally declined, so much that a

later chronicler could write that "there was no need to light a watch-fire on the boundaries of China."

The Mongols retained the written language established by their greatest medieval ruler, the tyrant Genghis Khan, but they were later politically divided. In 1921, the northern part of their sparsely populated but huge land mass declared itself the Mongolian People's Republic—a satellite of Moscow.

Over the years the Mongols in China were subjected to different local administrations. In 1947, the Inner Mongolian Autonomous Region, of which Huhehot is the capital, was established under Peking.

Even today there are more Chinese Mongolians outside the autonomous region of the People's Republic (1,200,-000) than in it (420,000). The population of Inner Mongolia has more than doubled from 180,000 in 1947. During the same time, officials admit, the total number of inhabitants in the autonomous region has grown from 3.16 million to 8 million. The bulk of them are Han Chinese—and this, demographically speaking, is what terrifies the Russians. They reason that if so many Han Chinese can swarm up to a border, why can they not swarm up beyond it?

The Inner Mongolians are no longer responsive to lamaism. Indeed, of ten Buddhist monasteries listed as extant in Huhehot in a guidebook compiled during the 1960's, only a portion of one remains—the five-towered pagoda of Wu ta si, a lovely little structure with Tibetan and Mongolian inscriptions. The others have been razed or remodeled for other purposes. And officials say that there is not one lama left.

However, the new faith of Communism has preserved a favored position for the Mongolians, honoring their phonetic language on a parity with Chinese and guaranteeing them 18-per-cent representation on all administrative bodies.

Slowly, the Mongolians are being converted from their nomadic life in yurts (felt tents) to settled existence in houses. Plague and syphilis have been eliminated. And, in addition to town physicians, there are 13,000 rudimentary "horseback doctors" to tend the pastoral clientele.

At the University of Inner Mongolia, the director of the Mongolian-language department, Chingertai, told me the hero of Inner Mongolia was a twentieth-century Mongol revolutionary named Sinilama, but acknowledged that Genghis Khan, despite his "class defects" and aggressiveness, had been a "great" man who unified his people.

There seems not the slightest reason to believe that the Inner Mongolians are attracted by or even pay much heed to the anti-Peking propaganda beamed from Outer Mongolia. The people are thriving for the first time in centuries. Just as their language is honored, so is their dress. In university classes I saw Mongolian girls and boys wearing lovely silk robes rather than drab Chinese costumes. Their excellent cuisine, music, dance, and folklore are carefully fostered. Though they have been considerably industrialized, their livestock population has quadrupled since Communism took over. The Mongolians rule the grassland from astride the long-maned little horses they ride so marvelously. Their summer horseback festival, called "Nadamu," is the year's great event.

The only obvious trouble is that, coddled and protected as they are, the Mongolians of the Chinese People's Republic make up less than 3 per cent of the entire population, although they are the eighth-largest national minority. If one considers that in just over a quarter century the Mongol population of the autonomous region has grown by only 240,000 while the Chinese population has grown by almost 5 million, one does not need to know Mongolian to read the handwriting of history on a fragmented lamasery wall.

As for the other minorities, one need only refer to the

implications of a moving scene I visited at Baishihu, near Huhehot. There, rising in a steep tumulus above the Mongolian plain that stretches endlessly from mountain range to mountain range is the tomb of Shao Jün, queen of the warlike Huns and one of the four greatest beauties in Chinese history.

Shao Jün was visited by the portraitist of a Chinese Han dynasty emperor who used to send his official artist around the country to paint the loveliest girls. The Emperor would then select the most beautiful to be his concubines.

Shao Jün was too poor to bribe the artist, and so he drew a most unflattering picture of her. She was brought to court as a mere lady-in-waiting, and was never even glimpsed by the sovereign. At length, the Prime Minister suggested that the Emperor send one of his daughters to marry Hohansheh, the uncouth king of the Huns, whose capital was near the modern Huhehot.

The Chinese ruler did not wish to send a daughter, so, instead, he promoted Shao Jün, whom he had never seen, to the rank of princess and betrothed her to Hohansheh. When she came to her first and farewell audience, the Emperor was so angry at his portraitist's gross misrepresentation that he had him strangled.

Shao Jün married the Hun in 33 B.C., bore him several children, and inculcated the habit of friendship and intermarriage among the border peoples. The year of her marriage was celebrated by imperial decree as "the first year of the frontier peace." Shao Jün was buried in what, because of its contrast with the dun-colored countryside, has come to be known as the Green Tomb.

The Huns went back to their favorite sport, fighting. They were smashed and dispersed by a Chinese general many generations later, and disappeared from Chinese scrolls. Meanwhile, they were riding westward, ending up eventually in Europe, where, as the Roman Empire crumbled, they settled in the Carpathians and on the Danubian plain and gave their name to Hungary. They were one of few peoples destined to emerge again in the world once they had disappeared from the almost eternal history of China, which had swallowed up and rendered nameless so many tribes before them.

The present-day People's Republic contains almost fifty officially recognized minority nationalities, comprising almost 50 million people, the approximate population of France or England. Today's Peking government specifically grants equal status to each minority, local self-government, and the freedom to speak its own language and to pursue its particular customs.

The ten largest, in order of size, are the Chuangs of Kwangsi Province; the Uigurs of Sinkiang; the Huis, scattered in many provinces; the Is of Yunnan and Szechuan; the Tibetans; the Miaos of Kweichow and Hunan; the Manchus of the northeastern region once called Manchuria; the Mongols; the Pu-i of Kweichow, and the Koreans on the border of North Korea.

Some of these peoples, like the Turkic Uigurs and the Mongols, speak Altaic languages unrelated to Chinese. Some, like the Islamic Uigurs and Huis or the lamaistic Tibetans and Mongols, had a different religious background prior to the spread of atheism. The culture of each minority is officially protected by the Nationalities Institute but subjected to Peking's interpretation of that status.

This policy of theoretically cherishing minorities is especially important for frontier peoples who, as in Sinkiang, Tibet, and Inner Mongolia, confront—in Soviet Central Asia, India's sphere, and Outer Mongolia—members of their own linguistic groups. Benevolence aside, the Chinese government sees the wisdom of keeping its border populations happy and immune to hostile propaganda. But the practice of this theory has not always succeeded in Sinkiang and Tibet.

It is interesting to note that the Nationalities Institute

has altered its program since the Cultural Revolution. Now, instead of teaching twenty tongues in the interpreters' course, it gives instruction only in Korean, Kazakh, Uigur, Tibetan, and Mongolian—each the language of a frontier people. Isolated minorities like the Chuangs obviously face the prospect of being Sinified and digested within the greater culture of China.

This is no question of coercion. Indeed, many little-known peoples, like the Tungs, are still being pampered. But Chinese-made goods, Chinese methods, Chinese media, and Chinese education either rival or surpass those of any of the fifty recognized minorities. And all religion is discouraged. Therefore, as so many times before, the stronger Han Chinese element must ultimately absorb the less dynamic cultures until they, like the Huns, disappear from China's recorded history. The difference is that, unlike the Huns, they will probably not reappear, but seem fated to vanish into forgotten folklore.

4

Uncle Sam
Joins the Game

The relationships between the United States, China, and Russia have been shifting constantly over the past thirty years. On August 23, 1944, Mao Tse-tung, who had not yet gained power but who was leading an ever-growing partisan army against the Japanese occupying forces, received John S. Service, of the U.S. State Department, in his temporary capital, Yenan.

"Cooperation between Americans and the Chinese Communist Party," Mao told him, "will be beneficial and satisfactory to all concerned. . . . China must industrialize. This can be done—in China—only by free enterprise and with the aid of foreign capital. Chinese and American interests are co-related and similar. They fit together, economically and politically. We can and must work together. The United States would find us more cooperative than the Kuomintang (Chiang Kai-shek's then dominant party). We will not be afraid of democratic American influence; we will welcome it. . . . America does not need to fear that we will not be cooperative. We must cooperate and we must have American help. . . . We cannot risk crossing you—cannot risk any conflict with you."

This, of course, was a tactical expression of improbable hopes. Chiang still controlled most of China, had a far larger army than Mao, and was backed not only by Roosevelt and Churchill, but also by Stalin. The next quarter century was to see the waxing and waning of Soviet friendship for the Chinese Communists, the development in Washington of a Manichaean approach to policy-making which consigned all Marxists, except Tito, to the devil, actual fighting between Chinese and American troops in

Korea, the verge of open war with China in the Taiwan Strait and Indochina, and eventually, on the part of U.S. interests and attitudes, a reconsideration of the relative importance to the world of Mao's hundreds of millions against Chiang's handful of followers.

Although an increasing number of Americans during the 1960's reflected on the potential advantages of recognizing what was then called "Mainland China," there were the emotional legacy of John Foster Dulles and the combination of the Korean War and subsequent near-wars with Mao to impede recognition. Then there was a formal U.S. commitment to Chiang, backed up by a huge investment in his armed forces and economy. To these were added the tensions arising from the U.S.'s ever-deeper involvement in Indochina, where a kind of containment policy was evolved, designed to keep pro-Communist Chinese factors from gaining strength or from sweeping southward toward Singapore in what was called the "domino theory" of power politics.

It took two major events to break this deadlock. The first was the split between Russia and China which put a halt to the Sino-Soviet bloc (although it took Washington years to acknowledge this); the second was the determination of a new U.S. administration to end our involvement in Vietnam and the neighboring sanctuary areas of Communist forces, thus easing China's own fears of American military pressures in its borderland. The entire process, which took some years to incubate, came to a head about 1969 when Chinese and Russian troops had a stand-off fight on the banks of the Ussuri River, which marks one of their common frontiers. It was clear that the break between Mao and the Kremlin was now irreparable.

By that time Richard Nixon was in the White House and, whatever case there is to be made against his domestic policies and the shabby men he chose to implement them, he had sensible and soundly based views on China and the peripheral questions frustrating improved relationships between Washington and Peking. In early November 1968, Nicolae Ceausescu, the independent-minded Communist boss of Rumania, told me that when he met Nixon in 1966, "he showed a real understanding of international problems. . . . I found that we agreed very substantially on China. We both thought there could be no solid basis for world peace until China was brought into it."

But once he entered the White House, Nixon had to move slowly. In February 1970, he told me that he wanted very much "to bring China into the normal international community." Later the same day, Richard Helms, a quietly intelligent man who was then the head of the C.I.A., told me that Washington was still confused about the Sino-Soviet situation, that the United States had the cards but did not know which way to play them, that it knew the talks between Peking and Moscow had been going badly, and that, although the Chinese had pulled their troops back from the disputed frontier areas, the Russians had refused to pull back theirs. This left Russia with approximately the same kind of choice that faced Israel after the Six-Day War. In February 1970, the Russians could have wiped out China. They knew that someday soon the Chinese would have a missile arsenal as well as nuclear warheads, and that then they would no longer have an overwhelming knockout, first-strike capacity. They wondered whether they should hit China while they could do so with relative impunity. As a result of all this, there had developed a triangular relationship in which we were inextricably involved.

These incredibly important issues claimed increasing attention in all the great capitals of the world, not just in Moscow, Peking, and Washington. In November 1970, Maurice Couve de Murville, who had been both foreign minister and premier of France, and who had just returned from a trip to China, assured me that "some day"

the United States would make a deal with China against
Russia. He was convinced that "that will be a policy. You
don't have a policy now." He insisted that the fate of
Taiwan was becoming more and more a Japanese rather
than an American decision, as, he said, they were beginning to realize in Peking. He thought from his own talks
with Mao, Chou, and others that China was more worried
about Japan than Russia was worried about Germany.

"The big thing," he concluded, "is for everybody to
learn the realities of China and forget old superstitions.
For 150 years, China was a colony of the worst sort.
Europe began its real colonization through Britain, which
fought the Opium War to force China's sale of opium.
Then the Taiping rebellion was opposed by Europeans in
order to squash any Chinese efforts to modernize their
country and to make it more independent."

By the spring of 1971, it was clear that a major shift in
United States policy on China was imminent. President
Nixon told me on March 8, in an interview he allowed me
to quote from: "Let us look at the world today. There are
two great powers facing us, Russia and China. They are
great powers and great people. Certainly neither of them
wants war. But both are motivated by a philosophy which
announces itself as expansionist in character. This they
will admit themselves. And only the United States has
sufficient strength to be able to help maintain a balance in
Europe and other areas that might otherwise be affected.

"What I am saying is not a cold-war philosophy. I hope
that we can further develop our negotiations with the Soviet Union. For, although we recognize that their ideology
is expansionist, they know what it means if the genie comes
out of the bottle and that their interest in survival requires
that they avoid a conflict with the United States. This
means that we must find a way of co-operating.

"For obviously pragmatic reasons, therefore, we can see
peace slowly shaping up. First, as we are doing, we must

end the war in Vietnam. We must continue our Soviet negotiations and open the door of co-operation to China. And in this way there will be a chance of building a world that is relatively peaceful."

It would serve no purpose here to go over the well-documented journeys and negotiations by which Nixon himself, through his ice-breaking trip to Peking, and also through his foreign affairs adviser Kissinger, reversed U.S. and Chinese policy. The whole episode is still fresh in the world's mind—especially Russia's.

Although Washington sacrificed important influence in Japan and at least a lingering friendship in India as it marched along steppingstones (above all, Pakistan) to Peking, it also managed wholly to rearrange the international power balance. China gained confidence, and at the same time America improved its bargaining position with Russia. Whether this compensated for the loosening of ties with Japan and Western Europe, a contemporary journalist cannot yet say. But one can, with some confidence, analyze the effects on China, not perhaps the strongest country on earth, but by far the largest.

The developing relationship between the People's Republic and the United States is compounded of logic and love, with considerably more of the former on the Chinese side and more of the latter on the American side.

The revolutionary logic impelling Peking to accept a friendlier stance toward Washington has its origin in the Sino-Soviet quarrel. Chairman Mao and Premier Chou must have felt that it would be folly to face two vast enemies at once. They decided to harmonize U.S. relations because they would be risking less than in any attempt to accommodate Russia.

This does not mean that China has ceased to oppose what it considers imperialist attitudes on the part of the United States. Peking is against any kind of balance of power and prefers the continuation of Soviet-American rivalry—so long as the United States does not get too weak. Chou frankly warns that Moscow and Washington "are contending for hegemony."

However, of the two, he fears America less. "U.S. imperialism started to go downhill," he has said, "after its defeat in the war of aggression against Korea. It has openly admitted that it is increasingly on the decline; it could not but pull out of Vietnam."

Vietnam plus the development of China's small nuclear arsenal have led to a more equal diplomatic colloquy. And President Nixon's signals were correctly and confidently interpreted.

In 1969, Nixon urged easement of tensions and stopped naval patrols in the Taiwan Strait. He resumed bilateral talks, lifted travel bans, and reduced trade embargoes. He also sent direct messages to Peking via General de Gaulle in France and President Yahya Khan in Pakistan.

The result was that Peking consented to a secret visit by Kissinger. Mao told Edgar Snow in December 1970 that if the Soviet Union would not point the way, then he would place his hopes on America.

At first there were hints that China wanted to accomplish this through the Democratic party as represented by Senator Mike Mansfield, who had indicated a desire to visit the People's Republic. But Mansfield postponed his trip, and the regime recognized that it was wiser to talk directly with the Nixon administration, even if it did represent "monopoly capitalists."

The wisdom of this decision was shown by the surprising personal rapport between Kissinger and the Chinese leadership. Chou told one journalist: "There is a man who knows the language of both worlds—his own and ours." And to an ambassador he said: "One can talk with Kissinger."

The traditionally xenophobic Chinese have been going out of their way to demonstrate friendship for Americans. They now recall that the United States, unlike Europe, never sought territorial concessions during China's disastrous nineteenth-century weakness, used its indemnification for Boxer Rebellion losses to build educational institutions, and sent missionaries who came to love China.

American visitors are not only feted, they are cautioned on the need to stay strong and alert to the Soviet military danger; also to repair existing differences with Western Europe to prevent its slow disintegration. Nobody taunts the United States with being a "paper tiger" any more. What is most feared is that we may become one.

But before détente can develop into formal friendship— like that between France and China—the U.S. will have to make some arrangement concerning Taiwan, in the end pulling out their vestigial forces and diplomatic representation. Right now, China regards Taiwan as France regarded Alsace-Lorraine before World War I—a lost province.

Kissinger knows this, of course, as well as anyone. But whether he will feel free to negotiate further diminishment of Washington's support for Taiwan in exchange for the further improvement of Peking relationships is still unknown. The administration is politically too weak at home to take excessive chances abroad.

Meanwhile, the United States is cautiously seeking to establish a new global power balance, and this China endorses for today but not for tomorrow. A United States no longer in Southeast Asia is no longer seen as menacing. Indeed, if anything, there is a worry that the war wounds in Vietnam plus Watergate may revive American isolationism at a time when only Russia could benefit from it.

From the Chinese viewpoint, good relations with the United States—while wholly different from those Mao discussed with Service in 1944—enable Mao to play a multifaceted foreign-policy game that was impossible as long as the People's Republic was isolated and alone in the threatening shadow of the Soviet Union.

China, it must be recalled, is not habituated to the idea of complex diplomatic maneuver, having for too many generations looked down its snub nose at all foreigners. Peking has never been an international city. Even now, despite China's steadily increasing world role, the foreign community is astonishingly small. There are only a few non-Chinese commercial representatives in the capital, and a handful of foreign newspapermen. The curious mixture of foreign residents includes an American doctor and a New Zealander, in China since the early days of Maoism, and an eccentric clutch of zealots, some British and some American, who got caught on the Cultural Revolution's fringes and found themselves paying for their ardor with imprisonment.

In the nineteenth century, a small "legation quarter" was created, and some of its largely old-fashioned buildings are now assigned to the countries who were the first to recognize the People's Republic. And Legation Street has been renamed Anti-Imperialist Street.

Newer diplomatic quarters for late-comers have been constructed in northeastern Peking. These quarters contain the U.S. Liaison Office and a large International Club, where diplomats and journalists often gather. The most pretentious establishment, that of Soviet Ambassador Vassily Tolstikov, the former Leningrad party boss, consists of an immense compound, heavily staffed, but virtually isolated, which scarcely any Chinese and few foreigners except citizens of Russia's allies ever penetrate. The U.S. Liaison Office is an interesting contrast. Although its thirty members are not on any diplomatic list and its chief, David K. E. Bruce, is not even acknowledged as an ambassador, it is recognized by the Foreign Ministry as both important and skilled.

Bruce, the only American who has ever served as ambassador to Paris, Bonn, and London, in all of which he was particularly successful, is Washington's outstanding diplomat—and the Chinese know it. Although the United States has no formal relations with Peking, Bruce's was the only Western diplomatic name mentioned in press accounts of the state dinner of October 1973 celebrating the national holiday.

Foreign policy does not feature prominently in Chinese publications. After all, for centuries China sniffed at all outsiders. The tradition of xenophobia is still strong, although it is generally masked by courtesy. Nevertheless, China's diplomacy is astute and the Foreign Ministry highly competent.

Having learned a bitter lesson from what China now refers to as the "negative experience" of alliance with Russia, the Chinese today base their policy firmly on the idea of independence. Those countries abroad that show independence vis-à-vis their own allies—for example, France and Rumania—are notably respected.

In seeking recognition as the leader of the so-called developing nations, the People's Republic subtly plays upon the rivalries between the two superpowers, despite its own developing friendship with the United States.

This play on rivalry is a tactic deriving from both Chinese tradition and contemporary circumstance. As Kuan-Chung Lo wrote in *Romance of the Three Kingdoms,* one of the world's oldest novels: "It is fitting to follow political changes and suit one's conduct to circumstances."

Mao might almost have had this in mind when he wrote his famous article of 1940, "Unite the people, defeat the enemy—a study on policy," which has been widely circulated since President Nixon's visit. It admonishes the Chinese "to make use of contradictions, win over the many, oppose the few and crush our enemies one by one."

The fundament of Chinese policy is therefore to remain wholly independent and at the same time to recognize that competition between Washington and Moscow "provides favorable conditions for the victory of the revolutionary people"—meaning the Chinese.

China today makes a great distinction between American and Soviet "imperialism." As the Chinese confided to the French in 1973: "The first is defensive; the second is offensive." What this of course means is that the Chinese no longer fear an American attack; they fear a Russian attack.

The Chinese want the U.S. to be alert to what they consider an alarming threat from Russia. Peking is determined to thwart Brezhnev's desire to forge an "Asian security pact" under Moscow's domination. It does not want to see the American military presence in Indochina replaced by the Soviets', and would certainly prefer to see all Southeast Asia neutralized.

China, furthermore, has no interest in U.S. attempts to limit the nuclear-weapons club. On the contrary, Chou told a French parliamentary delegation that "the more numerous the countries possessing the atomic bomb, the more distant the danger of war. The A-bomb is peace."

No matter how it differs from the U.S. on such questions as nuclear weapons or the future of the Middle East, China, for as long as it is at odds with Russia, will be impelled to seek common ground with the world's greatest capitalist state. And China expects to be at odds for a long time with Russia, which it sees as a revisionist-imperialist state and therefore a threat to its neighbors. As a country that shares 4,500 miles of frontier with the U.S.S.R., China has reason to remember how the Soviet Union invaded its own ally Czechoslovakia.

It is sometimes necessary for the Marxist mind to alter the ideological description of an enemy or potential enemy to make it conform to the ruling philosophy. This has most dramatically been the case with Russia, although officially Moscow is considered to have been a friend until Stalin's death, despite the unabashed opposition of Stalin to Maoist tenets, starting in the 1920's.

In 1950, Mao published an essay in which he urged "all Chinese without exception to lean either to the side of imperialism or to the side of socialism. Sitting on the fence will not do, nor is there a third road."

For years, "the side of socialism" was recognized as Moscow's. Nevertheless, Stalin often disagreed with Mao. He disliked the thought of the emergence of another Communist great power which might prove intractable.

Stalin intervened to ban a Soviet edition of a pro-Mao book. He sent his ambassador to Canton with Chiang Kai-shek's retreating forces in 1949. He forced Peking to accept the temporary presence of Russian troops in Port Arthur and Dairen.

Yet today Peking still officially contends that trouble with Russia started only after Stalin's death, that Khrushchev mocked Chinese agricultural communes and tried to make China knuckle under to economic pressures, that he unilaterally tore up a 1957 agreement on military technology.

Later he annulled technical and commercial accords, withdrew Soviet experts, and denounced the Chinese as "pure nationalists." In 1962, he furnished MiG's to India, which led directly to Brezhnev's policy of outflanking China.

This accumulation of events helped produce in Peking a desire to readjust international sights, a desire that did not go unnoticed in Washington. China altered its propaganda line to underscore Russia's "imperialist" tendencies, thus theoretically avoiding the "third road" barred by Mao.

One might say that Peking is reverting to its age-old policy of playing the "barbarians" (all foreigners have traditionally been seen as barbarians) off against one another. And this is all the easier to accomplish because the Soviet-American conflict is regarded as absolute, whereas such collusion as implied by Brezhnev's trip to the U.S. and the Middle East armistice is regarded as temporary and artificial. China's relations with the United States—and with Japan—are a direct reflection of its hostility to Russia.

The Chinese paint the Russian regime as nonsocialist. A girl schoolteacher in Shensi told me: "I teach that the

Soviet ruling clique are revisionists who threaten us. Years ago we were on friendly terms with the Russian people, but after Khrushchev came to power the Soviet revisionists turned against us."

The Russians, for their part, are anxious about China as a second Communist power and an ideological rival, and fear that 800 million Chinese may be demographically pushed into the relatively empty spaces of Soviet Central Asia and Siberia.

This concern seems specious when one considers that 80 per cent of China's own territory is still uncultivated. There should long be room in the People's Republic for a population whose growth rate is being deliberately slowed.

Moreover, in 1969, Premier Chou En-lai found with Premier Kosygin a reasonable basis for an agreement freezing existing borders; yet instead of following up on the agreement, Moscow increased its military strength along the frontiers. China responded in kind, and urged NATO to stay strong and ready.

Despite fears in Peking, and resulting official purges, there are probably not many influential Chinese officials who are secret Soviet agents. There are, however, some Chinese who are more sympathetic to Soviet methods than to American.

The army is alert to this. One high officer told me: "We must always ward off the influence of antiparty cliques like those of Chen Du-shiu [purged as a rightist in the twenties], Wang Ming [denounced as an "opportunist" in the thirties], Peng Te-huai [defense minister in the fifties], and Liu Shao-chi and Lin Piao."

Mao and his followers are determined that the army will never have political power, and this quite as much as suspicion of Soviet sympathies is perhaps what the present extensive purge of high officers is about. China is reasserting total party control over the armed forces.

In summing up, I believe it necessary to stress that it is a mistake to conclude that, simply because its relations with Moscow have soured, Peking now looks upon the U.S. as an amiable big brother with whom to line up.

Peking is not lining up with anyone. It opposes the "imperialism" of both superpowers, even if it now regards America as the lesser of two evils. Neither is Peking for international balance—especially a balance fixed by the superpowers for their convenience.

China itself made a play for Third World support in Africa and much of Asia in the 1960's and lost. Since then, however, it has made appreciable inroads, while the U.S. and Russia have lost headway—which does not exactly please either.

Russia sacrificed its huge foreign investments abroad with only partial recompense. Its position in Chile and Indonesia was smashed; its future in Cuba and India remains uncertain. For its part, the United States has lost ground in South America, South Asia, and Africa.

Whatever ultimately happens in the Middle East, with its crucial hold on industrial-energy supplies, the Third World is now increasingly conscious of its blackmail potential. It sees how it can confiscate Western investments and repudiate debts with little fear of retribution. Moreover, if it manages to unite permanently on a broader basis, it can play Europe, Japan, and the U.S. against one another to devastating effect.

But not China. As an autarky with modest long-range aspirations, the People's Republic depends minimally on the Third World for raw materials and markets, while, as a major aid-giver, it can help satisfy the Third World's need for outside help.

The satisfaction freedom has brought to most former colonies has been primarily psychological. Poverty, illiteracy, and instability have spread. The big exception, in a relative sense, is China. There literacy, both absolutely and relatively (unlike the situation in India), is on the upswing, and so is national pride. The living standard has risen without help from other countries.

The principal help China can give the Third World is its own example. There is an old saying: "Give a Chinese a fish and he'll eat for a day; teach him to fish and he'll eat for life." After many false starts, China is learning how to fish.

Venereal disease and prostitution have been eliminated; full employment has been brought about (at a sacrifice of potential per-capita productivity), massive reforestation has been stimulated, and, by disciplined mass effort, deserts have been rolled back. There is no energy problem because there are few cars and most people ride bicycles; yet they have ridden them all the way into the nuclear-missile age.

China's land-reclamation program is more valid for backward Turkey than Russia's or America's. Its classless, sexless egalitarian garb should attract India, with its outmoded economic and social caste traditions. Because the Third World contains most of the earth's population and acreage, the importance of Peking could someday be immense.

Japan today has the largest food-grain yield per acre (about 4,500 pounds), although it requires eighty-seven workers to provide this. The United States, fourth in per-acre yield, produces 3,050 pounds with only one worker. Neither China nor Russia is on the list of the first ten.

Peking has been right to opt out of the contemporary superpower race. It stands no chance of achieving any valid sort of hegemony this century. It probably falls even well behind nonnuclear Japan. But by entering the race for Third World leadership, it may achieve another kind of hegemony in the twenty-first century—leadership of 80 per cent of the earth's people.

Oddly enough, the program of the Sixth Comintern Congress, of 1928 in Moscow, agreed that "colonies and

semi-colonies . . . represent the world agricultural district in relation to the industrial countries, which represent
the world city."

And Lin Piao concluded, with a reasoning Peking still
adheres to, that the earth's poor, representing the "countryside," would overwhelm the industrialized state, representing the "cities." It is the Third World that Maoism
today sees as the critical unknown in the ultimate power
equation, though Chinese economists as well as those of
other nations see that the rich (industrialized) lands are
still getting richer while the poor lands (except those with
petroleum) have been getting poorer.

China hopes to build up its influence in the Third World
without war, which, now that it has fully comprehended
the secrets of nuclear weapons, it regards with proper
horror. Yet Moscow claims that in November 1957 Mao
calmly contemplated possible annihilation of 30 to 50 per
cent of the earth's population in an atomic war, since then
"imperialism would be destroyed entirely and there would
be only socialism in all the world." Mao did remark to
Nehru once that an atomic conflict might kill half— not all
—of mankind, but that "imperialism" would be razed and
the whole world become socialist. He thought that, as the
least-developed major power, China would have less to
lose thereby than the Soviet Union or the United States.
It is hard to know what to make of this now that Peking
has reclassified Russia as "socialist imperialist."

The Chairman now seems far more peaceful-minded
than he was in the 1950's and 1960's. Khrushchev claimed
that in 1959 Mao said to him: "You must provoke a war
with the United States, and then I will send you as many
divisions as you need: a hundred, two hundred, a thousand." "I explained to Mao," Khrushchev said, "that in
the present era, two missiles would suffice to transform
those divisions into radioactive offal. He told me there was
nothing to this. Apparently, he took me for a coward."

As recently as March 1966, when China's relations with

Russia had already soured, Mao forecast that war between China and the U.S. was "inevitable" and would break out within two years at most. "It is a mistake," he argued, still a prisoner of his old Stalinist reasoning, "to say that in the world today there are war powers and peace powers confronting one another; there only exist revolutionary war powers and antirevolutionary war powers. World revolution cannot come about by the evasion of war."

This cant has been eaten or forgotten in the wake of the altered power balance in which Russia has been replaced by America on Peking's ledger of friends. I should add that I cannot imagine the United States going to war against Russia on China's behalf and risking incineration by Russian MIRV's. Moreover, Washington must soon realize that, the fascination of playing political and diplomatic games in Peking aside, if it cannot rebuild its alliances with Europe and Japan, it will encourage Soviet freedom of action in Eurasia, including China, and decrease its own capacity to speak with influence in either Moscow or Peking.

But now, with infirm but constant alliances still valid between the U.S. and its NATO partners, and between the U.S. and Japan, the U.S. diplomatic position remains strong: indeed, it can now speak with Chinese backing on many things, especially in cases where Russia takes the opposite view. And, as Chou told me on October 26, 1973, "both the United States and China have sought to normalize their relations and to seek a common ground. President Nixon and Secretary Kissinger have opened up a new channel. The joint Shanghai communiqué [1972] shows that there are common grounds as well as differences. In this respect, the past year and a half have shown certain useful developments."

Uncle Sam has joined—or rejoined—the game in China. From the Chinese point of view, as well as ours, it was high time.

5

Getting Ready
for the Showdown

Earlier I have referred to Russia's game in China and have explained that for many years Moscow—even under the rule of Stalin—disliked and feared the thought that a dynamic and strong Chinese nation might develop on the Soviet border. The question rhetorically posed is: What do I mean by Russia's "game"?

The answer is simply that by hook or by crook, primarily by subversion and threat, the Kremlin plans as a matter of fundamental policy to insure that China is controlled by a co-operative, pro-Soviet regime, once Mao and Chou lose power, which is to say when they die. On an enormous scale, it is, I suggested earlier, the same kind of game being worked up by Moscow for Yugoslavia when Tito dies. But the problem posed by Yugoslavia, with its medley of disparate peoples and its relatively small size, is minuscule compared to that of China.

Obviously, the Chinese crisis is approaching rapidly, if for no other reason than the age of the two leaders who dominate the scene, Mao Tse-tung and Chou En-lai. And when that crisis comes, there is little doubt that the Russians will make all kinds of menacing gestures, marching their troops around and rattling their missiles. But I, for one, seriously doubt if they would ever contemplate deliberately launching a war to achieve their objectives. Not that they do not have ready and available the means for such an effort, and also contingency plans, but Soviet strategy today is based, whenever possible, on the reversal of Clausewitz's famous dictum: now policy is the continuation of war by other means, not vice versa.

Field Marshal Montgomery once told me: "There are

two rules of war. The first rule is never invade Russia. The second rule is never invade China." As far as the first rule is concerned, I am convinced Peking has not the slightest intention of breaking it. But it is, nevertheless, clearly preparing for the possibility that Moscow itself might violate the second.

There is no effort to hide this worry. In a Shensi village I saw a large poster on the main square showing Chinese troops fighting the Russians in 1969 along the Ussuri River. I saw the same picture in a textile factory in Huhehot, Inner Mongolia.

A high-ranking officer of the People's Liberation Army told me: "Political education in our unit stresses Russia, both in class struggle education courses and situation education courses." Another commander said: "We build tunnels, but the Russians talk about our threat. Tunnels are not aggressive."

And yet they constitute a main feature of Chinese preparation. I have seen tunnels everywhere, including one in a Peking factory, linked to the capital's extensive underground network, which displayed Mao's slogans: "Dig deep. Store grain everywhere."

Tunneling is an old Chinese stratagem. Mao's favorite strategist, Sun Tzu, who taught "the art of war" in 500 B.C., counseled: "The general who is skilled in defense, in effect, hides in the most secret recesses of the earth." All cities are riddled with underground shelters and connecting links. Tunneling is even regarded as an offensive tactic, and I would not be utterly astonished if portions of the Soviet frontier had been honeycombed by clever Chinese engineers.

Of another aspect of Maoist defensive strategy, the distribution of food and key supplies around the country, Chen Chung, of the Agriculture Ministry, said: "Each district must become self-sufficient in grain as a preparation against war. In wartime, communications can be cut."

People's China has a vast army, with limitless reserves. The full-strength division—volunteers who may be retained after their three-year term of duty—comprises somewhat over 10,000 men and has five regiments: three infantry, one artillery (twenty guns), and one armored (eighty tanks).

Training and small arms are first-rate; morale is high. Artillery relies heavily on the 120-mm. piece. But the air force, depending mostly on outmoded Soviet planes, is unimpressive. I saw plenty of these planes on airfields.

Maoism teaches: "Weapons are an important factor in war, but not the decisive one; it is man and not material that counts." Thus cunning (of which tunneling is an example), loyalty (insured by party control of the army), and guile are all vital instruments of Chinese planning. Sun Tzu taught: "All warfare is based upon deception." Chairman Mao wrote: "The Red Army generally operates by surprise attacks."

Nevertheless, the nuclear-missile age and the break with Russia have had a sobering effect. And as China has pressed forward its own nuclear-missile program, its leaders have, not surprisingly, come to respect atomic powers.

Mao says that no nation will really dare use atomic weapons, but there is an absence of ringing confidence in that assertion. As the Sino-Soviet split widened, China's nuclear-armaments program was given high priority, and is even now being increased at great expense.

During the last thirteen years, there have been fifteen test explosions, and the rate has accelerated together with deployment of operational medium-range missiles. It is China's steadily mounting nuclear potential that stimulates talk among Soviet hawks of the desirability of destroying it before it grows too dangerous.

There has been a perceptible thickening of Soviet forces stationed near China's borders, until now there are, it is estimated, nearly fifty divisions. There is, however, no special state of alert. My own feeling is that Montgomery's second rule will prevail—unless Moscow's policy-makers are tempted to attack by the possibility of an unstable situation in Peking.

China has always regarded itself as the great land power of Asia. The fact that Russia pre-empted that role, initially by seizing vast areas of China during its century of imperial decline, sharpened the dispute.

All Chinese rulers of the postimperial age have striven to restore their country's pre-eminence in land.

Chiang Kai-shek, during his brief governance, wanted to recover the lost regions just as much as Mao did later on. This is the one point on which the two old rivals never essentially disagreed. Like his non-Communist predecessors, Mao wanted the People's Republic to include all the provinces once ruled by the conquering Mongols, and not simply the smaller area claimed by the increasingly supine dynasties that followed them.

Indeed, all modern Chinese, despite present pretenses to the contrary, dream of restoring at least a good part of the territory confiscated from weak emperors by the Russians. However, there is still a wide range of discussion between maximalists and minimalists. Moscow might be surprised, even if it were someday able to install in Peking's Forbidden City a regime it regarded as friendly, to discover that the ousted Chiang spoke for a great majority when he wrote, in *Soviet Russia in China:*

"On October 12, 1929, there occurred the Chinese Eastern Railway Incident. Russian troops invaded Manchuli and Hailar in Manchuria and forced our local authorities to sign the Khabarovsk Protocol on December 22, another proof that Soviet Russia was continuing Czarist Russia's aggressive policy toward China."

The relationship between the two great neighboring countries had already been confused by personality disputes and individual changes of attitude long before the United States, during and after World War II, became directly involved. Stalin had sent two of his best military figures, Generals (subsequently Marshals) Zhukov and Chuikov, to help Chiang combat the Japanese.

Chiang himself sent his eldest son, Chiang Ching-kuo, to study in Moscow, where he remained more than a decade and married a Russian. On February 11, 1936, Chiang Ching-kuo wrote a letter to a Leningrad paper proclaiming himself a Communist and condemning his father as a public enemy. He has since returned to Chiang's side and will probably succeed him as titular chief in Taiwan; it is hard to forecast whether after that he will throw his lot in with Peking or Moscow.

Indeed, the Soviet Union, which after World War II suggested that Taiwan might be awarded to its suzerainty, has been playing a curious game there also since the split with Mao was formalized. It even sent on a visit a Russian journalist known for his close connections with the secret police, who had a visa personally approved by Chiang.

Peking, in the meantime, has pretended to modest territorial claims on the "unequal" nineteenth-century treaties that awarded Chinese lands to Russia. But, as Chou En-lai told me, "The Russians haven't even recognized objective facts like the existence of 'disputed areas.' In truth, using your phrase, their policy has been: 'What's mine is mine, what's yours is negotiable.' " The phrase in fact was coined by the late Charles E. Bohlen, the distinguished American diplomat and expert on Soviet affairs.

Of course, the argument over who is being modest and who is not cannot easily be judged. *Pravda* contends that in 1964 the Chinese formally claimed some 580,000 square miles of Russian territory, although they did not insist on immediate fulfillment. Mao counterclaimed that some Russians were demanding the immense but thinly populated province of Sinkiang.

During the period of sharpest superpower rivalry, above all while John Foster Dulles guided U.S. foreign policy, Mao seemed tempted to forget these territorial questions in order to reaffirm allegiance to the Marxist camp, then clearly dominated by Moscow. When NATO represented a strong "free-world" bloc led by Washington, the Chairman publicly acknowledged that China would "lean" toward Russia.

By February 1950, China had already signed new political, military, and economic agreements with Russia, establishing a kind of Peking-Moscow axis. From the Russian viewpoint, this not only removed China from the temptation of making any deals with the Western powers, but also encouraged it to forget its grudge against the Russian looting and pillaging of industrially vital Manchuria when the Japanese army there collapsed in August 1945.

The trend toward a new amity, founded on the ashes of inherited suspicion, was heightened by the start of the Korean War in June 1950 and by China's dispatch of large forces of "volunteers" when General MacArthur's army approached the Yalu River border. On October 1, 1950, Chou proclaimed that the Sino-Soviet alliance bound "nearly 700 million people" together. Two years later, he forecast that the friendship on which this pact was based would envelop every successive generation.

It became clear after Stalin died that, as is so often the case between neighbors with mutual territorial claims, the friendship was sorely menaced. After suspiciously watching Khrushchev's de-Stalinization program take shape in 1956 (with its obvious implications for Mao's even tougher rule), the Chinese officially charged the Soviet Communist party with making "unreasonable demands designed to bring China under military control." Two years later, Peking challenged Moscow's ideological and political leadership in the Communist bloc and elected to compete openly with Russia for leadership in the Third World.

Only later did the full extent of angry argument between Mao and Khrushchev become known. In 1954, Peking asked the then new Russian boss to disregard Russia's recognition of the "independence" and satellite status of the Mongolian People's Republic and, in effect, to hand it over to China. In 1960, six years after Moscow had spurned this proposal, Peking signed a treaty of friendship and mutual assistance with Outer Mongolia, something the Kremlin has been able so far to ignore.

That same year, Moscow not only reneged on a promise to send atomic-warhead prototypes to China, but withdrew all Russian technicians and their families, about 4,000 people, and destroyed the blueprints for pending industrial projects, including those for a gaseous diffusian plant, thus delaying Chinese nuclear advances by about three years.

From then on the die was cast. Russia had had only about twelve army divisions in the Far East, with five more in reserve, while the Chinese kept about twenty-four in Manchuria. Slowly these forces and their weapons were increased on both sides of the long border. The Russians began construction of an enormous new road and rail network and, as these came into being, deployed tactical nuclear weapons both in their own Asian provinces and in Outer Mongolia. They established a new command area—the Central Asian Military District—including 1,200 miles of frontier in Kazakhstan, Kirgizia, and Tadzhikistan—and moved its headquarters northeastward from Tashkent to Alma Ata.

Finally, as tension mounted, the two sides met in an armed clash on the obscure Chen Pao (Damanski) island of the Ussuri River in March 1969. Thirty-four members of a Russian patrol were killed. Shortly afterward a new battle ensued in which the Chinese are said to have lost eight hundred against the Soviet's sixty. Posters began to appear in China depicting the Russian army as an active enemy.

Kosygin and Chou met at Peking airport that September

to re-establish "normal" state relations on the basis of the "five principles of peaceful coexistence." But mistrust and hostility continued to grow, and Peking and Moscow began to compete for the friendship of their previous enemy, Washington, all the while edging ever closer to the verge of serious active conflict.

The main trouble area was the frontier region on both sides of the 4,500-mile dividing line—an area for the most part inhabited throughout history by non-Slavic, non-Sinic tribes and nomads. Turkomen of the U.S.S.R. are still ruled from Tashkent and other cities with large Russian colonies, much as the peoples of the Indian subcontinent were ruled by English colonists under the British raj. And the Chinese, pretending that Tibetans, Mongols, and Uigurs (formerly the majority in Sinkiang) are of consanguine stock, have immutably asserted their dominance.

But although minorities are officially cherished, provided they consent to abandon such old traditions as the lamaist Buddhism of Tibet and Mongolia, and accept Chinese sovereignty and Communist ideology, they are ultimately doomed to vanish in the enormous tide of Han Chinese culture and dynamism.

The minority tribesmen are doomed on both sides of the Sino-Soviet frontier. In 1970, Russia charged China with stirring up a pan-Turkmenian movement aimed at Soviet Central Asia. There were simultaneous indications that Russia was promoting a similar movement in Chinese Sinkiang and was paying an agent named Isa Yusuf Alptekin to go around the world on a "Free Sinkiang" propaganda tour.

There is no doubt that tens of thousands of Kazakhs and Uigurs have fled from Sinkiang into Russia in the last decade. As recently as 1973, the Soviet press accused China of "cruelly suppressing the national liberation movement of the Tibetan people" and other minorities in the name of "great-Han chauvinism." But it is just as likely that Peking is correct in calling the multinational Soviet state a "czarist-type colonial empire." I have visited both systems and come away with the feeling that neither the Uzbeks of Soviet Uzbekistan nor the Mongols of Chinese Inner Mongolia are anywhere near heading for room at the top.

This endless dispute is not likely, at least as I read the tea leaves, to produce an armed conflict between the two great imperial powers of Asia. There are, of course, hawks on both sides. In 1970, Soviet Marshal Ivan Yakubovsky warned that China was preparing for war, and Marshal Grechko demanded defenses in the east as strong as those in the west, most probably at the urging of Russia's military-industrial complex, which wants an excuse to keep defense expenditures at a high level.

For the past three or four years, it has been a common guess that both China and Russia were getting ready for a showdown. Would China make a weapons break-through, for example in the missile field? Or would Russia make a bargain with West Germany to insure a peaceful European frontier? Or would either side make a deal with the United States?

In one or another way each and all of these things have happened, so that the balance remains relatively unchanged. Chou says: "We think Western Europe is right to maintain its vigilance and avoid Finlandization." Nixon has visited both Peking and Moscow. And Russia's view still seems to be as Aleksei Adzhubei, Khrushchev's son-in-law, once said in an interview: "We do not have a conflict with the Chinese People's Republic but with the leaders of the Communist party of China."

Following his father-in-law's political demise, Adzhubei was quietly demoted, but his statement concerning Russia's quarrel with China's existing leaders remains true. It is odd that Moscow's insistence that Mao is a deviate from Marxist orthodoxy can be traced directly to the Soviet

party congress of 1956, where Khrushchev made his famous speech denouncing Stalin's excesses and his personality cult. There is little doubt that Maoism has developed
into a Chinese version of such a cult.

Mao certainly did not copy Soviet methodology along
his road to Communism. His effort to find a short cut by
the Great Leap Forward, featuring a hodgepodge of im-
practicable village industries, finally ended with a whimper
in late 1958, with Mao himself deprived of his office as
chairman of the republic. That job was awarded to Liu
Shao-chi, who lived to regret it. Mao did not enjoy being,
as he himself has described it, a "parent at his own fu-
neral."

Instead, with vitality remarkable in a man already old,
he struck back through the Cultural Revolution in 1966,
using the armed forces to give power to young Red Guards
who helped him regain total power—against the normal
party apparatus. Five years after this, Lin Piao, number-
one military officer in the country and minister of defense,
was purged, following Liu into limbo.

Mao has always insisted that "power grows out of the
barrel of a gun" and that the party controls that barrel.
He was forced by circumstance to point the gun at the
party during the latter part of the 1960's, but, once he had
achieved his goals, he reasserted civilian control of his
officers. And when the Red Guards became overexcited
and indicated a preference for radical leftists, symbolized
by Mao's own wife, Chiang Ching, Chou En-lai deftly and
swiftly took care that the relatively conservative faction
should reassert an upper hand in that uncertain period.

Mao, whose curious and original theory of continuing
revolution foresees recurrent cycles of disorder, was ready
for the Lin Piao conspiracy of 1971, in which Lin was
charged with actually seeking to murder the Chairman and
seize power. Later Mao let it be known, without allowing
the Chinese press to publish the news, that Lin had died

in the crash of a Chinese (British-built) Trident jet in Outer Mongolia on its way to the Soviet Union.

The plot gave the Chairman an excuse to purify the army leadership by weeding out those who might be pro-Russian, anti-American, or weak on Maoism. After all, Lin, once considered the most authoritative exponent of Maoism, had had a long period to install or promote his own men to key positions.

In 1968, because Russia had continued to deploy troops and weapons on the Chinese border, Mao wanted to be absolutely certain his forces would be loyal to him personally and to his own version of the Marxist credo, if and when a showdown came.

The convulsion that resulted in Lin's death and the massive military purge began in August 1970 when Mao announced: "Someone is seeking the state chairmanship and attempting to split the party." At first it seemed the "someone" referred to was Mao's own lieutenant, Chen Po-ta, who became the first known victim of the purification process, but before too long it was evident that the finger really pointed at Lin, despite the fact that the Defense Minister was an old colleague of the Chairman and had actually edited the famous Little Red Book himself.

Mao began his cleanup by naming to the top-level Military Affairs Committee men on whose loyalty he could rely and then reorganizing the Peking Military Region, which any hostile coup would have to capture. It was only afterward that Lin, his wife, and various followers were accused of fomenting a first counterrevolutionary plot in February 1971. Later in 1971, Mao personally assumed full command of the People's Liberation Army.

The great purge was completely logical in terms of Maoist dialectic. As he himself said in 1938: "According to the Marxist theory of the state, the army is the chief component of state power. Whoever wants to seize and retain state power must have a strong army." Of course, what he also meant was that he must have a loyal army. He made this plain when he "retained" state power against what he labeled Lin's threats to "seize" it.

As a result of Mao's cyclical theorem of recurrent revolutionary troubles, and even more as a result of the alleged plots by Liu Shao-chi and Lin Piao to grab control, the Chinese revolution—like Saturn and like all twentieth-century revolutions—has devoured a great many of its own children. Among the numerous top leaders and close associates of Mao who have either died or vanished since the People's Republic was declared in 1949 are the following (and this is but a short list):

Lin Piao, previously the Chairman's designated successor; Liu Shao-chi, once official chief of state; Peng Te-huai, former defense minister; Kao Kang, a head of the state planning commission; Lo Jui-ching, boss of the internal security forces; Po Yi-po, minister of finance; Lu Ting-yi, Central Committee chief of propaganda; Pen Chen, Politburo member; Ho Lung, an army marshal; Yang Shang-kun, Central Committee member.

The most dramatic purge, however, appears to have been that which followed Lin Piao's attempt to seize power on September 12, 1971. Among those who disappeared from sight with Lin were five other Politburo members. These included Huang Yung-sheng, armed forces chief of staff, and Li Tso-Peng, air force commander, as well as several other key party figures directly involved with military affairs.

The notable thing about the list is that almost all the men on it were connected with the defense establishment and most of them are known either to have been or to have been accused of conspiring in one or another way with Moscow and against the ruling Peking establishment.

Liu wanted to reactivate the Sino-Soviet alliance in the late 1960's. Peng was charged with communicating his dissident views to the Kremlin. Way back in Stalin's day, the Russians had been playing with Kao. Yang is said to have bugged his colleagues on the Russians' behalf; Lo is widely assumed to have been involved with the Soviet Union.

Even Lin, once considered the most authoritative exponent of Maoism, was driven by some force to mount a conspiracy (called by the code number 571) against the Chairman. It is officially claimed that the military was riddled with his sympathizers, that Moscow had pledged some kind of support.

It is perfectly obvious that Mao was convinced a plot was being mounted against him inside his own armed forces and among their spokesmen at the highest party levels, and, furthermore, from the tone of subsequent propaganda, that Russia was in some way involved, as either the inspirer or the sower of seeds in fallow ground. Mao therefore struck sharply, following his aforementioned precept that "the gun must never be allowed to command the party."

The command structure of the People's Republic does not yet appear to have recovered from the fearful shaking-up that followed the Lin coup attempt. At this time no new defense minister, chief of the general staff, or air force commander has been formally named to replace those purged.

Mao himself, as chairman of the party's Military Affairs Committee, is commander in chief, and Yeh Chien-ying, a marshal before all ranks and insignia were abolished in 1965, seems to be acting as defense minister. But the armed forces are still concentrating as intently on weeding out actual or potential anti-Maoists as they are on improving their equipment and training.

Geng Yü-chi, a deputy commander, told me: "By struggling against deviationists we can guarantee that our army won't change colors and become like the Soviet army which served the revisionist party of Khrushchev."

The Maoist leadership thus remains resolute in its determination to pursue the Chairman's very special path even though the Russian government and party, since Stalin's death, have been trying their best to change Peking's mind, or, failing that, to bring down the regime. And so, amid noisy propaganda blasts, under masks of secrecy, and behind immense troop concentrations, the Chinese revolution goes on with its purge.

As part of this change there has been a continuing shake-up in the armed forces. Eight of eleven existing military regions were given new commanders in 1973— the regions of Shenyang (including all Manchuria), Peking (including Inner Mongolia), Canton, Nanking, Wuhan, Tsinan, Lanchow, and Foochow. This massive shift does not seem to involve a purge but, rather, a complete reshuffling of responsibilities for the top troop commanders, presumably to prevent the growth of entrenched regional factions which could conceivably threaten the civilian hierarchy.

Apart from the top-ranking military figures listed above, a partial list of other senior officers who have been punished or shifted includes the following: Wang Pin-chang, deputy commander of the P.L.A. Air Force; Long Shu-chin, commander of the Sinkiang Military Region, which borders Russia; Cheng Wei-shan, commander of the Peking Military Region; Wu Fa-hsien, commander of the P.L.A. Air Force; Lan I-nung, first political commissar of Kweichow Provincial Military District; Chou Chih-ping, political commissar of Foochow Military Region; Chen Li-yun, political commissar for the P.L.A. Air Force of the Fifth Army; Nan Ping, first political commissar of Chekiang Provincial Military District; Wang Hsiao-yu, first political commissar of Tsinan Military Region; Wang Wei-kuo, political commissar of the P.L.A. Air Force for the Fourth Army; Huang Chih-yung, deputy director of the P.L.A. General Political Department; Liu Hao-tien, political commissar of the East Sea Fleet of the P.L.A. Navy; Wei Tsu-chen, political commissar of Kwangsi Provincial Military District; Li Tsai-han, political commissar of Kweichow Provincial Military District; Liu Feng, political commissar of Wuhan Military Region; Chiu Hui-tso, director of the P.L.A. General Logistics Department; Pan Fu-sheng, first political commissar of the Heilungkiang Provincial Military District; Liang Hsing-chu, commander of the Chengtu Military Region.

Also: Li Hsueh-feng, first commissar of the Hopei Provincial Military District; Yen Chung-chuan, deputy director of the P.L.A. General Staff Department; Liu Chieh-ting, deputy political commissar of the Chengtu Military Region; Wen Yu-cheng, commander of the Peking Garrison command; Chang Hsiu-chuan, deputy political commissar of the P.L.A. Navy; Huang Yung-sheng, director of the P.L.A. General Staff Department; Chang Jih-ching, second political commissar of the Shansi Provincial Military District; Tseng Kuo-hua, deputy commander of the P.L.A. Air Force; Li Tso-peng, first political commissar of the Kiangsi Provincial Military District; and Liu Ko-ping, first political commissar of the Shansi Provincial Military District.

I do not know how complete the above list is or just what form the purge has taken in each instance: death, incarceration, disappearance, disgrace, or simply loss of command. It will be seen, nevertheless, that key commanders from all three branches of the P.L.A. (army, navy, and air) plus general staff officers have been affected, as well as many notable political commissars, who play a vital role in the Chinese military system. The extensive weeding out of officers is comparable in scale (but not in brutality) to the famous Stalinist purges of Soviet officers falsely accused of pro-German sentiments.

It is evident that the leadership of the armed forces has been seriously upset and that there is no longer an outstanding commander on the political horizon who could challenge Mao for power as Lin is alleged to have done. Moreover, with Chou quietly reasserting an influence that is obscured only by the blazing sun that is the Chairman, the country has been restored to full order in the wake of the Proletarian Revolution, which rendered China giddy, and a new and friendlier relationship with the United States and Japan has come about.

Finally, it is evident that the Lin conspiracy, the military purification, and the relatively pro-American policy can be linked directly to Soviet policy, which is seen as continually preparing to threaten China through its troop deployment, efforts to achieve diplomatic encirclement, and attempts to stir up internal opposition to Mao. Whether the last is absolutely true or not, the Peking regime says it is true, and it thus becomes part of Maoism's current revealed gospel. Lin Piao himself was charged not only with having "illicit relations with a foreign power," but also, oddly enough, with having intended to "surrender to Soviet social revisionism, unite with the Soviet Union and the United States, and oppose China and Communism."

The international power balance will be crucially affected by the success or failure of Kremlin efforts to gain influence in China, either by carrot or by stick methods. There are hundreds of thousands of Russian soldiers stationed along the border and perhaps as many as a million Chinese positioned in depth opposite them. Both sides aim nuclear-tipped missiles at each other, although Peking's are much inferior.

However, despite rivalry between neighbors beset with old disputes, it could still prove easier for a post-Mao regime to follow a conventional pro-Communist and therefore pro-Soviet line than a relatively pro-American one.

At this juncture, nevertheless, all elements suspected of favoring a pro-Soviet posture are being eliminated from the Chinese power structure. This is particularly true in the P.L.A. The percentage of military men on the Central Committee elected by the Tenth Party Congress has declined by 12.8.

There is no doubt that the Brezhnev regime is now applying a massive squeeze on China, trying to encircle it while seeding it with pro-Soviet agents. Yet, while the Chinese regime is infuriated by these tactics and resists them stubbornly, it has offered a moderate formula for settling territorial arguments.

Premier Chou insisted to me that "with respect to the Sino-Soviet boundary, we never said that China wished to recover all the territories lost under the unequal [nineteenth-century] treaties. That is a rumor spread by the Soviet Union."

He recalled his abortive agreement of September 11, 1969, with Kosygin by which he accepted those treaties "as a basis" for negotiations, agreed to withdraw armed forces from border regions and then to arrange a new "realignment of the boundary, which we think would not be a difficult matter to settle."

Chou thinks Moscow is dragging things out "while waiting for other opportunities"—meaning new attempts to stir up trouble. The fact is that a reasonable outline for settlement exists and can be applied once the Sino-Soviet cold war ceases.

Through all this, Stalin's picture is still prominently featured in China's ideological Valhalla. Stalin's face could someday disappear from the gallery; but George Washington's would not replace it.

From the Chinese point of view, dealing with the United States these days is more or less like Lenin's dealing with the Germans at the time of the Brest-Litovsk Treaty negotiations at the end of World War I. Ultimately, China hopes to see the U.S. weakened; but it does not want it to go down the drain too fast, and it certainly hopes it will be on hand as a fire brigade against any Soviet assault on a naked and isolated People's Republic. It is plain that China will do its utmost to keep the U.S. and Russia at odds, whatever convenient interim periods of mild flirtation between the two may arise. China regards these as temporary flirtations of convenience whose importance need not be exaggerated.

For its part, and in the absence of a strong NATO, the United States is more or less forced to rely on China as a balance against potential Soviet hostility because political pressures both in the U.S. and among our NATO allies have steadily weakened the enthusiasm and vigor of that coalition. This dependence China welcomes, because even more undesirable to them than the weakening of the North Atlantic partnership on Russia's flank is the possibility of genuine Soviet-American co-operation.

Consequently, China has taken the new step of supporting all Japanese claims in the Kurile Islands seized by Russia (thus embarrassing Moscow); and even hinted in 1972 (which it clearly did not mean) that it might help Japan in a conflict with Russia. China proclaims to all Communist countries its opposition to the Brezhnev doctrine, under which Czechoslovakia was seized in 1968 and in which China sees the possibility that Russia might someday turn against it.

Despite all its efforts, China is technologically at least five years behind the Soviet Union and at least ten years behind the United States; it is the least industrialized of all the nuclear powers.

The Chinese testing area at Lop Nor and the gaseous diffusion plant at Lanchow were built with Russian aid. Several Chinese scientists were trained in Russia, which may have rendered them subject to suspicion later on. Lanchow has been producing uranium for warheads for more than a decade, and a reactor in Yumen has been making plutonium for a shorter period. It is reckoned that

China may now have many hundreds of nuclear devices. It certainly has many short-range missiles and four types of strategic missiles, MRBM's, IRBM's, and a still incompletely developed multistage ICBM. These, together with several hundred defensive SAM II antiaircraft missiles, about 1,500 fighter planes of dubious worth, and a strike force of MiG's and Ilyushins and an F-9 said to be capable of flying at twice the speed of sound, make up China's modern weapons systems. The French report that the Chinese have managed to soup up a locally manufactured version of the MiG-21 aircraft originally obtained under Russian license.

Thus, although China has almost incalculable reserves of trained conventional manpower, an immense paramilitary force, well-trained regular troops (some of which I have seen on maneuver), and a martial spirit (revealed to our embarrassment in Korea a generation ago), it does not yet have adequate means to make truly modern war. Given better jets, it could use the missiles it already has to destroy Far Eastern Soviet cities and targets like railway lines, but the punishment received in exchange could set the Maoist revolution back by decades.

However, Mao might very well have devised a strategy that takes these factors into account, in case his brinkmanship with Russia ever explodes over the edge. Should this one day be the case, and should the new diplomatic line prove ineffectual in deterring Russia, the Chairman may reckon, with De Gaulle (as the General confided to President Kennedy), that if he has enough A-bombs to "tear an arm off" an enemy, he can still prevent Russia from attacking. Indeed, André Malraux says Mao told him: "All I want are six atom bombs. With these bombs I know that neither side will attack me."

Of course, that is far too small a nuclear arsenal to serve as a preventive nowadays, and Mao knows this. But his arsenal has multiplied many times. Moreover, it is likely

Moscow no longer reckons it could achieve a successful pre-emptive strike against the People's Republic.

The People's Liberation Army may or may not be strong enough to rebuff a Soviet invasion. If Russia should some-day decide to take the terrible risk of simply standing off and blowing up China with its long-range missiles, concentrating on nuclear-development plants, it could theoretically get away with it—unless the resulting political explosion involved the whole world. But the P.L.A. is quite strong enough to change the political power in Peking, above all after Mao's death, and to either aid or block Sino-Soviet understanding.

This is what the extensive purge and all the political maneuvering since China's Cultural Revolution are about. The Russians have counted on eventually inserting a pro-Russian group into Peking's leadership and once they have gained control of the Chinese party, as Adzhubei more or less said, they feel sure they could change its policy to follow Moscow's concepts of orthodoxy, ideology, and convenience. Indeed, the Russian ambassador in Peking, Vassily Tolstikov, previously party boss in Leningrad, always displayed calm confidence in the future of Sino-Soviet relations—until the Lin Piao plot exploded, and Lin disappeared. After that he became increasingly pessimistic and somber. In line with this development, noted by Tolstikov's diplomatic colleagues, one of Moscow's principal envoys in Europe has said indiscreetly and more than once: "When Mao Tse-tung is no longer boss of China, things will change and we will have better relations with Peking."

The Peking gossip mart, mainly tenanted by foreign diplomats and journalists, has recently been buzzing about a struggle in the shadow of Mao between so-called right-wing and left-wing factions of the Chinese Communist party.

This terminology is variable. Sometimes it is used to distinguish those who wish to improve relationships with the United States in order to bolster China's position in the deadly rivalry with that other superpower, Russia, from those (it is officially stated) who, like Liu and Lin, either prefer Moscow or at least oppose accommodation with Washington.

In other cases, it is used to distinguish political figures close to the Chairman, like Premier Chou, who insist on maintaining a certain stability in state policy, internal and external, from others, like Mao's wife, Chiang Ching, who are often associated with opposition approaches within the hierarchy. These latter are said to be even more violently revolutionist than the dominant faction that is directing the government now.

It is difficult in China to speak with certainty of such goings-on within the highest circles. The Chinese are known not only for masking their feelings and voicing their opinions by indirection long after an event, but also for their extrasecrecy, imposed by a highly authoritarian regime.

Nevertheless, the groups most frequently spoken of in both connections—"American" versus "Soviet," and relative stability versus even more revolutionary activism— are commonly said to center around Chou, in the first instance, and Chiang Ching, in the second instance.

Thus, in the unusually abstruse argument now current with respect to the conservatism of that old sage Confucius, it was often thought the initial attack on Confucianism was intended to embarrass Chou.

More recently, it is believed the Premier was able to bolster his position and divert the thrust against Chiang and her supporters by stressing the "educational" aspects of the discussion. All this is too subtle, and too Aesopian in its implications, ever to occur in any Occidental land.

During late September and early October 1973, observers speculated that arrows in the local media were being aimed against Chou and that Mao's wife was holding the bow. This may have been true. But the same observers changed their analysis when Chiang began slipping in party rankings, and there were indications that her supporters had failed in their objective—if such it was—of pulling down the Premier. As long as Chou remains the number-two figure in China, China is going to remain politically friendly to the United States and politically hostile to Russia.

Chou went out of his way, when talking to me, to stress that Watergate had not ruined America's status in the eyes of Chinese officials and that Kissinger continued to be highly regarded. Also, while saying it would be easy to settle the Sino-Soviet problem on the basis of his own 1969 understanding with Premier Kosygin, he again went out of his way to call Russia "imperialist" and "fascist," a country threatening peace and masquerading as "socialist."

He was not exactly kind in everything he said about the U.S., but on the relative scale of superpowerdom, as analyzed by Peking, the U.S. does not come out too badly. And he no longer used the word "fascism" when talking about the United States.

What happens when he and the Chairman are both gone is by far the biggest question today in China. (Mao and Chou are not the only very old men in the leadership; three of the five party vice-chairmen are in their seventies.) It is a question important not only in terms of a vast country's internal administration but also in terms of the whole international power balance.

When the time comes for new men to replace the gerontocracy, we will at last know if Mao has really solved his long-term problem by insuring that the leadership following him will remain true to his ideas and will avoid the temptations proffered by Moscow. There may have been real Soviet agents among those purged in recent years, but others, like Liu Shao-chi, probably only admired Russian methods and industrialization and perhaps were only looking for a renewal of massive help from Russia. It is unlikely that those removed after Lin Piao's fall either had real connections with the Soviet armed forces or had been charged with fake documents like those Stalin used against Tukhachevski and his colleagues in 1937.

The big question thus shakes down into several questions. Will the Russians acknowledge, when Mao dies, that in recent years China has improved its nuclear capacity enough to make military action too costly? Will the new diplomacy practiced by Chou succeed in keeping a NATO force strong enough in the West to attract sufficient American support for China in the East to exclude the possibility of a Soviet-initiated conflict? Finally, will the Chinese army be absolutely loyal to the next regime?

My guess is that the Kremlin prefers that its role in China in the next few years should not take the form of military invasion. Rather, it will back secret supporters in the People's Republic committed to installing a pro-Soviet regime. This is what European observers say Russia has in mind for Yugoslavia when Tito dies.

The Chinese are already suspicious of the Kremlin's plans. Chou recently claimed that a "chief of the Soviet revisionists" boasts: "Sooner or later, the healthy forces expressing the true interests of China will have their decisive say"—meaning that a pro-Moscow faction will take over.

Undoubtedly Russia is furious at its failures and obsessed with an ultimate Chinese "threat." As one Russian told me in Peking, the Russians mistrust the Chinese as total "dogmatists" who insist a thing is "black" or "white" just because Chairman Mao says so. The fact that this system is also practiced in Russia is conveniently forgotten.

But although Brezhnev has increasingly numerous divisions deployed near China, he would probably invade it only to "restore order" in the event that civil strife was provoked by his agents. Decidedly inferior in nuclear equipment, the Chinese could still blast a few Soviet cities; they could use their huge conventional army and labyrinth of civil defenses; and, if resolutely led, they would be prepared to bleed copiously for victory.

Should Russia attack while the present government rules, it risks major defeat unless it just stands off and atomizes Chinese cities. In that case, it would certainly lose some of its own towns, as well as international respect, and possibly touch off world war.

But if it sticks to fomenting internal ruckus while brandishing an external sword only as an implicit threat, it can hope to get away with things, which is why China is trying so hard now to purify the political leadership of its armed forces and to arrange an orderly succession to the Mao-Chou tandem.

The two most likely successors to Mao seemed to be Li Teh-sheng, a party vice-chairman in his sixties, and Wang Hung-wen, another vice-chairman, who at thirty-nine is the Politburo's Benjamin. Also in the running is Chang Chun-chiao, chairman of the Shanghai Revolutionary Committee, a man in his late fifties said to be Chou's favorite; and Yao Wen-yuan, also from Shanghai, said to be close to Chiang Ching, whose prestige, however, is faltering. Even Li has recently lost influence.

Whoever wins the succession stakes will have to stand in well with the army. Whether any of the above leaders already has the requisite military prestige cannot be assessed. If there is a period of doubt or if all pro-Soviet seeds have not yet been rooted out, that would be the time for Brezhnev to make trouble.

Everyone must ask if Maoism can survive the death of Mao and, in so doing, avoid giving up its special individuality to Soviet ideological pressures. Paradoxically, Mao has made the People's Republic both more and less able to face this test: more, because he has launched it on a new and modern road, and less, because he has deliberately chosen to insure that Chinese society should always be stirred into continuing ferment.

In the end, human beings are human beings, and it is hard to imagine any of the species surviving indefinitely in such a bubbling crucible. Mao has already led his followers through the period of a Hundred Flowers, which largely wrecked the remaining intellectual infrastructure; the Great Leap Forward, which unbalanced industrial recovery; and the Cultural Revolution, which for a time set army against party and both against the universities. These were perhaps romantic experiments, but they were costly.

Mao himself has simultaneously confirmed and denied Sun Yat-sen's theory that Chinese are less interested in religious or philosophical struggles than in becoming emperors. He assumed virtually total charge of his countrymen, then allowed himself to lose power. In 1966, he launched a cunning movement to recapture it.

He has been defamed by his detractors as non- or even anti-intellectual and unoriginal, an indifferent calligrapher and a mediocre poet in a land where both arts are venerated. But De Gaulle's and Churchill's opponents also often belittled their creative talents. The fact remains that Mao Tse-tung has demonstrated the flexibility and survivability of his leadership. Here one may do well to recall that Stalin won his political battle against the more blazingly brilliant Trotsky and Bukharin. What we now await is proof that Maoism without Mao can survive a contest against Stalinism without Stalin.